THE
BUY TO LET

Aberdeenshire Library and Information Service
www.aberdeenshire.gov.uk.libraries
Renewals Hotline 01224 661511

THE
BUY TO LET
MANUAL

THIRD EDITION

How to invest for profit in residential property
and manage the letting yourself

TONY BOOTH

howtobooks

Published by How To Books Ltd
Spring Hill House, Spring Hill Road
Begbroke, Oxford OX5 1RX, United Kingdom
Tel: (01865) 375794. Fax: (01865) 379162
info@howtobooks.co.uk
www.howtobooks.co.uk

First published 2003
Reprinted 2003
Reprinted 2004
Second edition 2006
Third edition 2008

British Library Cataloguing in Publication Data
A catalogue record for this book is available from the British Library

ISBN 978-1-84528-252-3

Produced for How To Books by Deer Park Productions, Tavistock
Typeset by PDQ Typesetting Ltd, Newcastle-under-Lyme, Staffs
Printed and bound by Bell & Bain Ltd, Glasgow

NOTE: The material contained in this book is set out in good faith for general guidance and no liability can be accepted for loss or expense incurred as a result of relying in particular circumstances on statements made in the book. Laws and regulations are complex and liable to change, and readers should check the current position with the relevant authorities before making personal arrangements.

Contents

List of Illustrations

Preface

Being a landlord has gained greater public acceptance today than at any other time in history. More people have achieved financial security in recent years and many have chosen to invest in or have inherited a second property. Letting is recognised as a reliable way of profiting from a second home and the practice has now become commonplace throughout all sections of society.

Latest figures show that 25 per cent of all new mortgages taken out during 2006 were for a buy-to-let purchase, which represents an increase of 57 per cent on the previous year. Investors took out 330,000 new buy-to-let loans worth a staggering total of £38 billion. This recent, rapid and continuing escalation in the volume of rented properties – and consequently the number of landlords – is fundamentally transforming the face of letting in England and Wales. The process was kick-started by changes in legislation almost two decades ago.

The 1988 Housing Act was introduced by government to help fuel the rented sector by providing landlords and their tenants with a balanced degree of security. It created regulations to protect the landlord's income and guaranteed they would regain legal possession at the end of tenancy. It also provided tenants with good quality, safe housing and a defence against being evicted during the tenancy term.

With help from a stable and healthy economy and the resulting higher disposable income enjoyed by many, the residential letting market grew quickly. Although owner-occupiers are still in a majority, renting is seen as a viable and sometimes preferred alternative for many people. However, the modern landlord frequently lacks the experience, knowledge and time needed to deal efficiently with their property and tenants. Some jump in with both feet, blissfully ignorant of the laws affecting them, only to find themselves in deep and turbulent water within a very short period. It is perhaps not surprising that many resort to paying a letting agent to deal with the tenancy and, although some offer a very competent service, many fail to provide their clients with the personal care and attention ultimately desired.

This book intends to equip the reader with everything they need to know about buying and preparing a suitable investment property. It also explains how to find good tenants, where to obtain forms and how to complete tenancy agreements; it deals with deposits, rent arrears and the process of regaining possession. More importantly, it will help achieve compliance with the extensive volume of legislation affecting landlords in England and Wales. In short, it is a comprehensive but concise guide for the would-be, go-it-alone landlord wishing to avoid agency fees by creating and managing their own tenancy.

After 20 years of being a landlord and operating as an estate agent and letting agent, I have concluded that knowledge provides much more than power . . . it allows the person possessing it to work efficiently, knowing they are armed against the pitfalls of ignorance. Minor hiccups will inevitably occur but having a sound foundation in the standard of property being let, finding good tenants and having a comprehensive tenancy agreement all help reduce the risk.

By empowering yourself with the information in this book, you will enjoy the financial and personal rewards that becoming a landlord can provide. You will also have the satisfaction of knowing that you are in full control of who will occupy your most valued asset and for how long, the rent they will have to pay and the conditions they will need to observe. The private rented sector is an exciting, stimulating and challenging arena for novice and professional alike; this book will guide you through its many facets and show you how to generate a considerable income, even if you are currently employed in another occupation.

Throughout this book please note that for ease of reading the term 'landlord' refers to either gender and to one or more people or to a company.

Tony Booth

Website: **www.tonybooth.info**

Acknowledgements

As always, thank you to my trusty band of proofreaders who have advised, suggested, criticised and edited much of the content of this book. I am particularly indebted to Chris Park and Alan Lancaster for giving freely of their time and expertise. Special thanks to Professor Peter Robson of the Law School at Strathclyde University, whose assistance in validating the chapter on Scottish law is much appreciated, and to the Scottish Executive for their help and advice.

CHAPTER ONE

Identifying a Suitable Property

In this chapter:

- ◆ recognising properties that are in demand
- ◆ researching local trends and facilities
- ◆ the potential of an investment property
- ◆ assessing leasehold restrictions
- ◆ avoiding a HiMO property
- ◆ essential elements to increase letting potential.

If you have yet to buy a property then you are in a very advantageous position as you can locate and purchase a unit that you know will be in demand. The only restrictions are likely to be the availability of such units and having enough funds to buy one. Failing to make a profit from letting is usually the result of poor planning and inadequate preparation. Many landlords make the mistake of trying to provide accommodation that is unsuitable for the area and only later discover there are not enough tenants available to maintain a high occupancy rate. The secret is to accurately identify the location, size and style of property in highest demand and then endeavour to supply it.

RECOGNISING PROPERTIES THAT ARE IN DEMAND

Identifying your client group

There are two ways to do this depending on your personal circumstances and the preferred type of property and tenant.

- ◆ If you already have a preferred location, research the area thoroughly to assess the most likely type of tenant; this will help identify the most suitable type of property.
- ◆ If you have already decided on a particular type of tenant, examine where those tenants are most prevalent and buy appropriate property in that specific area.

In both situations, it is best to consult local estate agents who also operate as letting agents. They will advise on the best area to consider and the type of tenants seeking accommodation within it. This advice is usually free as they will

1

see you as a potential future customer. Use their expertise as it could considerably increase your future profit margin. The following information may be helpful if you remain uncertain about your target client group.

Students

Students often seek low-cost accommodation close to their college or university and cohabit to reduce the burden of rent. This can be problematic if one of the group later decides to leave during the tenancy. It may be the students' first experience outside the parental home and the taste of freedom may result in excessive noise, untidiness and damage to property and décor. Landlords should consider supplying robust furnishings and ensure a parent acts as guarantor. Properties are likely to be in high demand during term-times only and may remain empty for periods in between. Before supplying student lets, confirm with the educational institution that a need exists for private sector dwellings as many provide their own subsidised accommodation on campus or nearby.

Tenants with young children

Terraced and semi-detached houses will be in high demand amongst this group providing they have adequate space and a safe enclosed garden area. Properties meeting the needs of a growing family are ideal, particularly those located near a school, recreation space, health centre and neighbourhood shops. Good public transport routes are also often desired.

The unemployed and/or those in receipt of housing benefit

Bear in mind that *anyone* can become suddenly unemployed and may therefore need to apply for housing benefit. That said, supplying specifically to those in receipt of benefit is *not* a course advised for the novice landlord. The benefit system is very complex and fraught with problems. Even experienced landlords are often frustrated by delayed benefit payments, unhelpful local authority staff, red tape and bureaucracy. Landlords are advised to obtain information from the local authority about housing benefit and to consult experienced landlords through local forums or associations.

Employed young couples

By far the greatest number and diversity of tenants seeking rented property of all types are young single people or couples in full-time employment. This is the ideal group to target as there will be fewer problems encountered before, during and at the end of a tenancy. The type of property best to supply will vary according to:

- employment opportunities in the area
- the income and aspirations of tenants
- and the facilities afforded by the neighbourhood.

Elderly tenants

In general, elderly tenants focus on different elements from younger people when looking for rented accommodation. Matters important to them will include:

- ease of access
- good and courteous neighbours
- security and safety
- good public transport
- and plenty of local facilities all within easy reach.

In contrast, properties:

- above the first floor with no elevator
- located in an area with a high crime rate
- with a younger age population
- or lacking security measures

are likely to discourage the elderly. This is a good group to target if a suitable property can be found, as most elderly tenants:

- care for their accommodation
- pay their rent in full and on time and
- tend to repeatedly renew contracts over a long period.

The disabled

The term 'disabled' encompasses a wide group of people, many of whom are poorly catered for in the private sector. This gap in provision can be filled successfully and profitably by landlords prepared to meet the needs of this group. Approach the local authority, social services, nearby hospitals, and also any appropriate charity or agency, to assess the level of demand and appropriate requirements.

Remember that, in providing a property to this group, you will have to ensure it is adapted to meet the needs of the individual and that it conforms to both local and national guidelines for health and safety (you or the tenant may be entitled to grant-aid for any necessary adaptations).

Young professional high-earners

This is a good group to target if you can acquire the right property in a sophisticated and fashionable area or a luxury residence close to a city centre. Young professional high-earners (YPHEs) rarely rent for more than two or three years in any location because they have a career strategy and frequently pursue improved positions elsewhere in the country. However, whilst occupying your property they are prepared to pay a high rent and will care appropriately for the accommodation. The only problems to consider are that YPHEs:

♦ have high expectations about the quality and location of the property
♦ are concerned about the calibre of furnishings and standard of decoration
♦ will demand a superior level of service from you as their landlord.

Any faults reported must be dealt with fast and efficiently. The initial capital outlay for a suitable property will be considerable but, given its location in a good area, it should achieve above-average capital growth by the time you sell it. Meanwhile, you can anticipate a reasonable return through letting.

Company lettings

Consider targeting major employers in the region with details of your property. With a company let it is the business that is named on the tenancy agreement instead of an individual person. This type of tenancy has several advantages for the landlord:

♦ rent payments are usually made promptly by bank standing order
♦ tenancies are often renewed over several years
♦ any damage is usually dealt with quickly and professionally.

Companies invariably look for well maintained units at competitive rents and with a superior management service. A company letting can pay dividends if you and your chosen property can fulfil these requirements.

RESEARCHING LOCAL TRENDS AND FACILITIES

Buying close to home

If possible, choose a property near to or within easy reach of where you live. Apart from giving you some peace of mind it also means you will:

♦ have good local knowledge to answer tenant enquiries
♦ be within easy reach for viewing appointments, emergency repairs and to undertake regular inspections of the property
♦ recognise when the area is deteriorating to assess the best time to sell.

Local information

Find out all you can about the neighbourhood where you are considering buying property and try to match the facilities available with your chosen client group. It is rare to find an ideal *property* in a perfect *location* at an acceptable *price*, but confirming the greatest number of positive elements under each heading will produce mutually satisfying results for you and your future tenants.

Supply and demand are the greatest influences involved in letting. They affect the length of time a property will be let (without void periods) and the rent achievable. Assess demand by talking to letting agents who will have a unique insight into their area. Assess supply (and any potential over-supply) by looking at 'to let' boards in the neighbourhood and advertisements in local newspapers. Check the same boards and adverts weekly to see how quickly properties are being let.

Ask the local authority planning department about new developments under construction or any that are being proposed. What changes are likely to take place in the locality? Will they adversely affect your ability to let a property nearby?

Examine the number of major employers in the area and identify any proposals for land redevelopment. A new hospital being built will attract a growing local population. Staff will need somewhere to live and this increase in demand could sustain your property for several years. Conversely, a factory announcing closure might be symptomatic of a local recession. Property may be devalued as a result and there could be an over-supply of rented accommodation in the long term.

THE POTENTIAL OF AN INVESTMENT PROPERTY

Apartments -v- houses

If the demand exists and you are able to quantify it, invest in an apartment rather than a house. The main reasons for this are:

- apartments attract a mobile population and are always in high demand, particularly in city-centre areas;
- apartments require less maintenance, reducing annual expenditure;
- apartments are usually less expensive to buy and easier to sell;
- upper floor apartments are more secure during void periods;
- apartments generally occupy less space and therefore require less furniture, carpets and equipment;
- a garden will require attention during void periods; an apartment balcony will not.

However, bear in mind:

- in rural areas, small family houses with a garden may be in higher demand than apartments;
- apartment blocks may have a service charge for maintenance and common area upkeep which will have to be paid whether the property is occupied or not;
- the enjoyment of an apartment is dependent on there being thoughtful neighbours above, below and to each side;
- the cleanliness, decoration and general condition of the external aspects and communal entrance hallways will be controlled by the management company, whereas with a house the owner is usually directly in control;
- apartment owners are often prohibited from letting their property by the lease (but see below).

Investment property

'Investment property' is a title often given to dwellings that need considerable repair. They may appear attractive to the novice landlord simply because of their low price but buyers of this type of property need to be aware that:

- A comprehensive survey is essential before submitting an offer, so that all defects are identified and realistic costs of repair can be obtained from contractors.
- There will be a void period from the day of purchase to repairs being completed when no income will be earned. Despite this, there may be charges to you as the owner for council tax, electricity, gas, service charge and/or management fees, which will have to be paid from personal funds.
- The property may be in a run-down area with neighbouring properties in a comparable poor condition and this will reduce the long-term letting potential.
- It may be difficult to obtain a mortgage, as most lenders will not want to accept the risk of repairs not being completed. Any loan granted is therefore likely to be low and the lender may also require additional security.
- The investment property may be classed as a HiMO (see below) and lack the minimum fire-safety and other standards required for such dwellings. Some landlords are now disposing of these properties, with vacant possession and at a low market value, to evade the long-term improvement costs.

ASSESSING LEASEHOLD RESTRICTIONS

Leasehold properties

Where a property is leasehold, the owner ('lessee') must abide by the conditions of the lease. Leases are usually for a term of 999 years (or the remainder of) for older properties, but can be for the remainder of 99 or even 50 years for many newly built inner city dwellings. Once the lease expires, the property ownership usually reverts to the headlessor. Mortgage lenders are often reluctant to advance a loan for any purchase where the lease is 50 years or less because the property value reduces according to the shortened lease-term remaining.

The lease should always be thoroughly inspected *before* purchase as many prohibit letting. If such a clause exists, write to the headlessor and enquire whether owners are allowed to conditionally let (or more accurately sub-let). When an arrangement of this type is made, there is sometimes an additional charge to the owner which may be a single or an annual payment or a charge per tenancy. Bear in mind that these additional expenses reduce annual letting profit.

The lease may also prohibit your tenant from keeping pets, disturbing neighbours with noise after a certain time, erecting a satellite dish or TV aerial, and many other restrictions. As the owner, you will be responsible for *ensuring* your tenants keep to these conditions.

AVOIDING A HiMO PROPERTY

Houses in multiple occupation (HiMOs)

The novice landlord should be extremely cautious before contemplating the purchase of a 'House in Multiple Occupation (HiMO)' – or of letting an ordinary house and, by virtue of the manner in which it is let, allowing it to become a HiMO. The problem is that this type of property must conform to a vast array of rules and regulations, some of which are nationally enforced, others are specified by particular local authorities.

The Housing Act 2004 introduced a stringent regime of safety requirements and management procedures that some owners of this type of property must comply with. Failure to do so can be considered a criminal offence and attract a fine up to £20,000. Local authorities have been granted tougher new enforcement powers and a new definition of a HiMO was introduced. This states:

'House in Multiple Occupation' means a building, or part of a building (e.g. a flat):

◆ which is occupied by more than one household and in which more than one household shares an amenity (or the building lacks an amenity) such as a bathroom, toilet or cooking facilities; or

◆ which is occupied by more than one household and which is a converted building which does not entirely comprise self contained flats (whether or not there is also a sharing or lack of amenities); or

- which comprises entirely of converted self contained flats and the standard of conversion does not meet, at a minimum, that required by the 1991 Building Regulations and more than one third of the flats are occupied under short tenancies.

And is 'occupied' by more than one household:

- as their only or main residence, or
- as a refuge by persons escaping domestic violence, or
- during term time by students, or
- for some other purpose that is prescribed in regulations.

And the households comprise:

- families (including foster children, children being cared for) and current domestic employees,
- single persons,
- co-habiting couples (whether or not of the same sex).

The above definition describes many let properties and, once a property is defined as a HiMO, landlords must comply with the complex array of regulations or risk facing dire consequences. Local authorities have the powers to close a property down and/or inflict heavy fines on those failing to comply.

The Housing Act 2004 also introduced mandatory licensing for certain types of HiMO. These include those comprising three storeys or more that are occupied by five or more persons, who comprise two or more households. It is prudent to note that a loft space, attic or basement *capable* of being used for residential purposes will be considered as one storey in the calculation. Some local authorities also operate landlord accreditation or registration schemes for HiMOs that do not automatically have to comply with mandatory licensing.

The 'Housing Health and Safety Rating System (HHSRS)' was introduced under Part 1 of the Housing Act 2004 as a replacement to the prior Houses in Multiple Occupation (HiMO) fitness test. HHSRS is a new approach to the assessment of risks to health and safety in residential premises. Local authorities will in future base enforcement decisions in respect of all residential premises on the basis of assessments under HHSRS.

For more information consult the Environmental Health Officer or Housing Department of the local authority region in which the property is located or the area you intend purchasing. Also, obtain a copy of the *Housing (Management of Houses in Multiple Occupation) Regulations 1990* from The Stationery Office (TSO), telephone customer services on 0870 600 5522 for details or obtain online at **www.opsi.gov.uk**

There is an excellent website at **www.landlordzone.co.uk** for additional reading on this and other relevant subjects and for an overview of the regulations. The Department for Communities and Local Government was established in 2006 and its website has a wealth of valuable information for HiMO landlords, including various Statutory Instruments detailing the new regulations introduced under the Housing Act 2004. This set of data can be accessed at **www.communities.gov.uk**

ESSENTIAL ELEMENTS TO INCREASE LETTING POTENTIAL

There are specific elements of a property that increase its letting potential. Although these will vary according to the individual location and certain tenant groups, many are universally desired by those seeking new accommodation. Examine the following and attempt to acquire a property combining most of the components listed (not in any preferred order):

Houses	Apartments
attractive location	attractive and fashionable location
private and safe garden	well-maintained communal grounds
secure garage	secure garage or designated bay
double-glazed windows	double-glazed windows
modern kitchen and bathroom	modern kitchen and bathroom
gas central heating	gas central heating
separate shower cubicle	quality soundproof timber flooring
quality alarm system	quality alarm system
spacious living room	above ground floor
log or coal-burning fire	some storage space
south-facing garden	south-facing balcony
conservatory	lift access to upper floors
original quality features	modern hi-tech features
neutral décor	neutral décor
fitted bedrooms	fitted bedrooms
guest WC	en-suite shower
good commuting position	good public transport route
quiet roads (safe for children)	close to or in a city centre location

Who is selling and why?

Find out as much as you can about the seller and do not be afraid to ask why they are selling. The owner will be aware of any adverse conditions affecting the neighbourhood (and the property) and, although they are unlikely to freely divulge this information to a potential buyer, the way they respond may suggest you should be more cautious about proceeding.

An effective method is to knock on a few doors of neighbouring properties and politely explain that you are considering a purchase. Ask if they would be prepared to advise you about any known problems with the area and properties in it. The information given by this method has proved invaluable in my own property investments; in my experience, first-hand local knowledge should always be considered paramount when planning a purchase.

Supply and demand

Although every purchase should be assessed on its own particular merits, it is an established fact that apartments are much more popular with the mobile population of many inner city locations. Career-oriented young professionals require the flexibility and ease provided by an apartment. Some also enjoy the status symbol of chic and fashionable style living that a modern apartment bestows on its occupier. Others just want the freedom to socialise away from their accommodation rather than in it – space becomes irrelevant and less is preferable for these busy individuals.

Houses gain in popularity out of city centres. Additional living space and a garden become important elements for couples that have or are planning to have a family. Others aspire to live on their own 'estate', without having to take into account or be potentially irritated by those living above or below them.

Supply and demand is perhaps the most crucial of all considerations when deciding whether to invest in a particular type of property. They are location-specific qualities and thorough research before purchase is essential. Bear in mind that because apartments are more popular and more profitable, developers build more of them – check with local letting agents to assess whether an oversupply might exist in a particular area. Experienced agents will also suggest the type and size of property to buy and where to invest to get the best returns, particularly if they think they may be employed to let and manage the unit after it has been bought.

The days have long passed when the price of an apartment was generally less than that of a house. Style, size and location are now primary value-driving factors, particularly within inner city boundaries. Fashionable high-rises and des-res conversions outclass and out-cost many of the more traditional family style homes, so the conventional theory that apartments are exclusively for the financially prudent no longer applies. Whilst cost will always be a major consideration, if not *the* major consideration, the issue of which is cheaper to buy is more blurred these days. One point worth remembering is that whilstground floor apartments cost about 20 per cent less than those on upper floors, they are perceived by tenants as being less secure and are therefore lower in demand and more difficult to let. As a result, the initial saving on capital outlay may not cover the losses created by frequent void periods occurring over time.

Selective licensing

Some local authorities have begun enacting new rules granted to them through the Housing Act 2004, which allow them to operate a selective licensing scheme for *all* private sector landlords (not just those that own Houses in Multiple Occupation). The cities of Salford and Manchester were the first in Britain to enforce the regime and fears are that it will quickly spread across all regions, so check the situation with your own local authority before buying a property you intend letting out. Whilst acquiring and complying with a licence may not pose a problem for diligent landlords, the added cost and bureaucracy could blight a buy-to-let investment.

Selective licensing is permitted in areas where rogue landlords are believed to operate and/or where anti-social behaviour is known to be prevalent. The idea is that licensing will help control both these elements for the betterment of good landlords, neighbouring owner-occupiers and tenants. The average cost of a licence is £500 per property and landlords applying must meet the minimum standards required by the particular local authority. Operating without a licence in an area where one is required can result in a fine not exceeding £20,000.

SUMMARY

- Choose a location that is popular for letting and with an abundance of eager tenants.
- Identify your target client group, learn their housing needs and supply them.
- Apartments are more popular than houses, particularly in cities, but find out what type of property people are looking for in your own area.
- Read any lease governing the property thoroughly before purchase to find out whether letting is prohibited.
- Take into account the full and real cost in time and money to undertake repairs and improvements to an investment property.
- Be cautious of buying a HiMO.
- When choosing a property to buy, assess whether it has enough good qualities to optimise its future letting potential.

CHAPTER TWO

Buying the Property

In this chapter:

- ◆ estimating running costs
- ◆ assessing and forecasting the yield
- ◆ taxation
- ◆ buying with tenants in occupation
- ◆ surveying the property
- ◆ finding a competitive mortgage
- ◆ investing with substantial existing capital
- ◆ timing is everything!

Having found a property, you need to examine its income potential more carefully and consider the options for buying it. Rushing in will simply invite disaster. Bear in mind that, once you have bought the property, it must work *for* you, not *against* you! Take your time and research thoroughly. Make a plan of how you intend to proceed. Consider matters such as:

- ◆ funding
- ◆ instructing a solicitor experienced in let property
- ◆ obtaining a survey
- ◆ making essential repairs
- ◆ assessing rental income after expenses
- ◆ undertaking legally required inspections
- ◆ buying furniture and equipment
- ◆ acquiring tenants and obtaining references for them.

You should only consider submitting an offer to purchase if you feel confident about the above elements.

ESTIMATING RUNNING COSTS

It may be difficult to identify all the costs associated with letting a property *before* purchase, particularly if it has not been let before. Some expenses may have to be estimated and a rent level calculated from limited information.

The exercise is nonetheless essential if you are to quantify the income-generating potential of your proposed investment. Remember that it must make a reasonable profit after all deductions to produce a favourable income. Failing to do this could mean squandering time and effort on an unproductive venture.

Occupied running costs

'Occupied' running costs are items you will have to pay with tenants living in the dwelling. These include:

- ◆ Mortgage payments.
- ◆ Lender's authorisation fee (letting is usually prohibited by mortgage lenders but permission may be given subject to a charge per tenancy term).
- ◆ Accountant's fees.
- ◆ Bank charges.
- ◆ Legal charges if a solicitor deals with the tenancy agreement, otherwise the cost of purchased forms (allow £50 a year).
- ◆ Tenant referencing.
- ◆ Minor repairs (allow ten per cent of rent over 12 months as a mean average).
- ◆ Council tax if the property is a HiMO.
- ◆ Water charges (normally paid by the tenant but some water companies impose the charge on the landlord; check with the water company for your area).
- ◆ Replacements and renewals for carpets, furnishings, fittings and equipment (allow ten per cent of rent over 12 months).
- ◆ Building insurance (some policies do not offer cover to let property and block policies offered through service-charge payments rarely provide adequate protection to landlords).
- ◆ Landlord's contents insurance (some policies do not offer cover to let properties or between tenancies or for those considered to be a high-risk, for example HiMOs and student lets).
- ◆ Any management or service charge payable (the owner/long-lessee is always liable, it is rare for management companies to provide for the sub-tenant to meet such charges).
- ◆ Gas-safety inspections which are legally required and must be conducted by a CORGI (Council of Registered Gas Installers) engineer.
- ◆ Electrical safety inspections (ideally conducted prior to each tenancy term or otherwise annually). A five-year check of wiring and system installations is considered good practice.
- ◆ Other expenses, such as the use of a car to get to and from the property, telephone, postage, stationery, photographs for inventories, copying keys and photocopying manuals and documents.

Unoccupied running costs

'Unoccupied' running costs are items you will need to pay when the dwelling is empty. These are likely to include:

♦ Gas and electricity charges for heating and lighting (heating will be needed in cold weather and lighting will be required for viewings and/or whilst undertaking maintenance). Allow two monthly payments per year.

♦ Council tax (at a reduced rate for empty properties). Allow two monthly payments per year.

♦ Interior decorating and exterior painting (a considerable expense if a contractor is hired).

♦ Cleaning (labour and materials); allow for pre-tenancy and post-tenancy cleaning. Allow for professional carpet cleaning every two years.

♦ Gardening (when the property is empty). Add an element for the upkeep of any garage, outbuilding, fencing or walls.

♦ Tenant advertising (or tenant-find agency charges).

♦ TV licence (if a television set is provided).

Estimating the rent level

Complete the following three exercises:

1. Invite local letting agents to view your property and assess an appropriate monthly rent. This service is usually free of charge as they will hope you will employ them.
2. Examine local newspapers to see what rents are being advertised for similar properties in the area.
3. Walk around the neighbourhood and identify any 'to let' boards. Obtain the full details of each property and note the rent of any dwellings comparable with the one you are proposing to purchase.

From this you should be able to make a realistic estimate of the appropriate rent for your property.

ASSESSING AND FORECASTING THE YIELD

'Yield' is a term used by property investors to calculate the profitability of different dwellings in the letting market. Most landlords recognise two distinct types of profit involved with property: short-term '**income from letting**' and long-term '**capital growth**'. The yield, expressed as a percentage, takes both into consideration to provide a comprehensive assessment and 6 per cent to 9 per cent is acceptable to most landlords.

With the information obtained so far, you can calculate the yield with the formula in Figure 1.

$$\frac{\text{(a) Net Letting Profit (after tax)}}{\text{(b) Current Property Value (less selling costs)}} \times 100 = \text{(c) Yield (\%)}$$

Fig. 1. Yield calculation.

Enter the data you have obtained into the document below. Repeat this for each property.

INCOME	Year 1	Year 2	Year 3
(a) Rent anticipated per month			
(b) Number of months per year the property is likely to be let			
(c) Rental INCOME per year ('a' multiplied by 'b')			
EXPENSES			
Mortgage (interest element only can be offset against tax)			
Lender's administration fees			
Accountancy fees			
Bank charges			
Legal fees including tenancy forms			
Tenant referencing			
Minor repairs and maintenance			
Council tax (if a HiMO)			
Water charges			
Replacements and renewals			
Insurance			
Management/service charge			
Gas and electrical safety inspections			
Void period gas, electricity, council tax, water, TV licence			
Painting and decorating			
Cleaning			
Advertising			
Gardening			
Other: travel, postage, stationery, keys, photocopying			
(d) Total EXPENSES			
(e) Taxable profit ('c' less 'd')			
(f) Tax at __% =			
(g) PROFIT AFTER TAX ('e' less 'f')			
YIELD (divide 'g' by the current saleable value after deducting all estimated selling costs, then multiply by 100)			

Fig. 2. Record of forecasted profit.

Yield can change from year to year according to the value of the property, the rent obtained and the level of expenses incurred through letting. By applying this approach to several properties you can identify which is the better buy at any particular point in time.

Professional investors forecast the anticipated yield over several years and you can also attempt this by taking advice and making considered judgements about expenses, tax liability, rental income and property value. The ambition of all speculators is to see the yield rise above the best interest-rate return from a bank or building society or other forms of investment. Buying a low-maintenance property in a good area, at a competitive price and with the qualities required to produce a good letting income, will help to achieve a yield of between seven per cent and ten per cent.

The calculation models described in this section are examples only, given for guidance. Other models with variable formulae may produce different results. It is not possible here to take into account the various elements which may be pertinent to your personal circumstances.

TAXATION

Income tax

You will be liable to pay income tax on the profit made from letting, after deducting any allowable expenses. The way tax is calculated will vary according to personal circumstances, any additional sources of income and other elements influencing your financial situation. You should:

- ◆ Make contact with your local tax office at the earliest opportunity, explain your plans and seek advice. The tax office will help you estimate the tax you are likely to pay from letting.
- ◆ Keep all receipts, paid invoices and any relevant documents relating to the property, as these will be required when completing your accounts for HM Revenue & Customs. Keep a record of the date paid, how it was paid and brief details of the service or materials bought.
- ◆ Consider employing an accountant *before* you buy the property. An experienced and qualified accountant will be able to offer you good advice and save you money in the long term.
- ◆ Take a course on book-keeping. You need to know how to keep adequate records for both HM Revenue & Customs and for your accountant. Presenting your records properly will also help to reduce accountancy costs.

- On the internet, HMRC's own website at **www.hmrc.gov.uk** offers lots of useful advice and a list of local offices. **www.yahoo.digita.com/taxcentral** includes a tax calculator, up-to-date news, information relating to taxation, and a question and answer forum.

Capital gains tax

Capital gains tax (CGT) is not usually payable on an individual's own home. It is, however, payable on most let property. You are liable to CGT on the profit made from selling it, that is, the capital remaining after deducting the original purchase price and accounting for personal allowances and permitted expenses whilst owned. CGT rules change occasionally. Your accountant will advise you about the current situation and suggest the best arrangements for buying the property to reduce your eventual liability to CGT.

BUYING WITH TENANTS IN OCCUPATION

Proceed with extreme caution if considering the purchase of a dwelling with existing tenants. Give regard to the following:

- Obtain copies of the tenancy agreements and any notices issued. Consult a solicitor experienced in the legal aspects of letting to confirm that agreements have been properly completed and conform to current Housing Act legislation.
- Obtain copies of the inventories, gas safety certificates, any record of electrical safety inspections, and any other appropriate documentation relating to the property and occupiers.
- Obtain the original referencing results and ask for details of any rent arrear history.
- Confirm that the current occupiers of the property are those named on the tenancy agreements (for example, has a vacated sharer been replaced or has a tenant now got an unidentified partner living with them).
- Identify the term for each tenancy (it may affect your ability to gain vacant possession if no term exists or one has expired).
- Read the tenancy agreements, giving particular attention to landlord obligations and facilities to increase rents.
- Meet the occupiers and satisfy yourself that these are the type of people you would have chosen as tenants.
- Check whether the tenants paid a deposit and, if so, whether it has been protected as required by law in one of the approved schemes. Don't rely on the landlord's information alone – verify the situation with the tenants.
- Should you decide to buy with tenants in occupation, consider using a reputable and knowledgeable property development professional. Internet

users may wish to visit **www.istone.co.uk** to assess the services they offer to would-be landlords.

Buying with existing furnishings

It may appear advantageous to buy a property already furnished and equipped. However, it will be uneconomic if furnishings and equipment are of a poor quality and/or do not comply with current legislation. Read Chapter 3 before proceeding, otherwise you may find yourself paying additionally for disposal costs.

SURVEYING THE PROPERTY

Inspecting the fabric of the building

As an estate agent, it often surprises me that so few people inspect properties thoroughly before buying them. Don't allow the seller to intimidate you. Remember, they are asking you to hand over a considerable sum for their property. Take your time and scrutinise the building thoroughly. When inspecting:

- Take notes about any adverse observations.
- Be prepared for every eventuality: take a small pair of step-ladders for access to the roof space, binoculars to view the exterior and socket-testers to check for faulty wiring (available at most good DIY stores).
- Check all window frames internally and externally for rot and confirm that they all open properly.
- Look for condensation between the two panes of glass with any double-glazing. This is evidence of a broken seal.
- Check all accessible water-pipes for leaks and confirm that pipes and tanks in the loft or in a cellar are lagged.
- Inspect baths, basins, showers, toilets and cisterns for cracks, dripping taps, leaks, poor seals, mould-growth and other damage. Turn taps and extractors on to ensure proper operation. Give particular attention to the area beneath hot and cold water tanks where staining may indicate an ongoing or old leak.
- Gently tap ceramic tiled walls to identify any that are loose.
- Pull back carpets where possible to assess the condition of the flooring.
- As you go through a doorway, close the door to ensure it fits correctly in the frame.
- Inspect ceilings for bowing as this is a sign of loose plaster. Look also for leakage stains.
- Examine the exterior for blocked, damaged or missing sections of guttering; broken slabs or paving that rises above the damp-proof course; missing or damaged roof slates; crumbling brickwork and receding mortar joints; damage

to boundary walls or rickety fencing; and look inside any garage, shed or outbuilding.

Arranging for a survey to be undertaken

Once you have conducted your own in-depth inspection of the building and are reasonably content with its condition, invest in a more professional and comprehensive surveyor's report. Before proceeding check with your mortgage company, as many require you use an approved or in-house surveyor.

If you are happy with the results, consider employing an electrician to check the property's electrical system (see also Chapter 3). It is also prudent to employ a plumber to inspect water-pipes, taps, stop-cocks, radiators, tanks, pumps and boilers.

FINDING A COMPETITIVE MORTGAGE

There is a vast array of mortgages available and the variation can be very confusing. The Financial Services Authority (FSA) is the independent watchdog set up by government to regulate financial services and protect the rights of the public. It provides a free, plain English *Guide to Mortgages* which can be obtained by writing to them at 25 The North Colonnade, Canary Wharf, London E14 5HS (telephone 0845 606 1234 or visit **www.fsa.gov.uk/consumer**).

Once you have decided the best type of mortgage, you can start searching for one that provides the best value. The internet is an easy way of obtaining up-to-date information and you can access thousands of loans offered by lenders throughout the country. If you are able to let your computer do the walking, try these sites:

www.moneysupermarket.com for advice on the best-buy mortgage in various categories. Their *Rate Alert* system updates you by e-mail when a better interest-rated mortgage enters the market.

www.moneyextra.com/compare/mortgages to search through over 8,000 different mortgages.

www.yourmortgage.co.uk supplies mortgage information and current 'best buy' details with advice for the self-employed.

www.mortgagesexposed.com is a quite extraordinary website offering a free on-line or downloadable book covering every aspect of the subject.

One alternative to using the internet is to consult a mortgage broker. There are mortgages not generally advertised and better deals that a broker has access to. They will identify a selection that best meets your circumstances. Brokers charge for their services so find out what fees are involved before employing one. A list of mortgage brokers can be found in *Yellow Pages* or consult your accountant who may be able to recommend a local one to you.

How To Books have published *Save Thousands Buying Your Home* by Maxwell Hodson. This is an excellent reference and guide for anyone considering a property purchase. Alongside useful money-saving information, it offers the reader realistic, sound advice on how to obtain the lowest mortgage and arrange finances so you get the best deal.

Before accepting a mortgage, obtain written confirmation from the lender that letting is permitted. Some completely prohibit renting. Others may have strict rules about the category of tenant, the type of tenancy agreement and the method of management. There are also often mandatory fees payable to mortgage companies for granting a tenancy and these are best identified in advance so you can include them in any profit forecast.

Buy-to-let mortgages

In recent years, lenders have recognised that many people wish to invest in property intended for the letting market. Some have devised products specifically tailored to would-be landlords (called 'buy-to-let' schemes). The concept was originally promoted by ARLA (the Association of Residential Letting Agents) whose members reported a gap in the availability of mortgages for their client landlords. Buy to let packages, varying in nature, can now be obtained from many high-street lenders, including most banks and building societies.

The advantages include:

◆ The letting income generated by the property forms part of the decision-making calculation by the lender for granting an advance.
◆ Lenders are usually prepared to consider granting a mortgage, even though the applicant may already have one running on their own home.
◆ Those who are self-employed (or intending to be full-time landlords) and those otherwise unemployed are not usually obstructed from making an application.

The disadvantages include:

◆ Lenders usually require a significant amount of information about the property and forecasted data on the anticipated rental income.
◆ It may be compulsory to accept various insurance policies from the lender.

- ◆ The tenancy agreement must be drawn up by a solicitor or through a recognised agency.
- ◆ It is often mandatory to employ a letting agent approved by the lender to oversee the creation and management of the tenancy.

For more details about buy to let, visit ARLA's website on the subject: **www.arla.co.uk**. Alternatively, consult any high-street bank for details of their package and shop around because schemes vary from one lender to another.

The buy-to-let mortgage product market has grown substantially and lenders are now seeking new ways to attract would-be landlord investors. Some have abandoned the restrictive monthly rent to mortgage repayment formula and are now offering loans that are equal to or in excess of rental income. Despite the temptation, this is an extremely perilous financial enticement and landlords are advised to consider carefully the level of debt they are prepared to accept. It is widely accepted that when interest rates exceed five per cent many buy-to-let schemes become unaffordable, because rents rarely increase enough to compensate for the added outlay burden. It is therefore essential that investors consider the effect that rising mortgage rates could have in the future and do not accept a level of debt that could ultimately cripple them.

The wise buy-to-letter will incorporate a buffer into their strategy that allows for at least one or two months in the year when the property will be empty and void of rental income – and a margin that provides some breathing space should mortgage rates increase beyond what may already be anticipated.

INVESTING WITH SUBSTANTIAL EXISTING CAPITAL

If you have substantial capital, you may be tempted to buy a property outright without considering the advantages of a loan. You may believe that full ownership is safer, easier and more rewarding, as it will negate third-party involvement and minimise complications. Whilst all of that is true ... you could also be reducing the potential return from your investment! With capital of between £100,000 and £200,000 or more, you are able to enter the realm of the serious let-property investor and achieve potential high returns from a process known as **gearing**.

As the term implies, gearing is a means of *getting out* more than you *put in*. It allows you to acquire more properties through planned and careful investment, using the capital to obtain additional funds. The more properties in your portfolio, the more income can be generated through letting *and*, by buying the right properties and selling them at the right time, the more capital growth you can make. The more capital you have the more you can invest ... and so on. Some of the most successful millionaires have made their fortune this way.

There is a higher degree of risk involved, but then the potential returns are higher too. Success lies in the breadth of knowledge and experience that the investor has about property in general. They must have an eye for dwellings with potential for capital growth and understand when it is right to buy and wise to sell. They need a sound business plan and access to skilled financial advisors. They must also be capable of accepting risks in their investment strategy.

When gearing is used to good effect, a yield of up to 20 per cent or more can be achieved, given an element of luck in finding the right properties in the right location, purchased at good prices and sold when local values are at their highest. Add to this low void periods, good tenants, high rents and prolonged low interest rates, and the return on capital can be multiplied several times over. Always bear in mind that gearing brings a better return when the total yield plus capital growth exceeds the borrowing rate, that is, the cost of acquiring funds.

Experienced investors also use 'interest-only' mortgages to maximise the effect of gearing. Currently, only the interest element of mortgage payments are accepted by HMRC as allowable deductions against annual income tax, which means the yield gained from a buy-to-let can increase through an interest-only loan. In addition, monthly mortgage payments tend to be lower, so there is a double bonus to such a strategy.

However, with an interest-only mortgage, the repayments are entirely made up of 'interest' with nothing paid off the capital – which means the entire amount of the original loan will have to be paid at the end of the term or when the property is sold (whichever happens first). This strategy makes an assumption that the property will increase sufficiently in value to meet the debt amount at the point of disposal. Although many accept this as a reasonable risk – consider the situation of falling property prices, as happened during the 1980s and early 1990s. Gearing with an interest-only loan is really only worth considering if an investor can afford the potentially disastrous consequences of an economic or property recession.

www.mortgagesexposed.com provides access to a free book on buy-to-let, which includes a chapter on 'gearing'. This is the best plain English explanation of the subject I have found in recent years. For more in-depth reading, you may wish to obtain *Buy to Let Secrets* by Richard Davies and Neil Lewis, which offers comprehensive and stimulating information on the topic (JoJaffa Ltd. Tel: 020 8715 3525).

My own book, *The Beginner's Guide to Property Investment* (ISBN: 978-1-85703-961-0) is a useful resource for novice buy-to-letters embarking on their first purchase. Whilst the content is aimed at first-time buyers, it also deals with a wide variety of different property investments and will help you avoid the most common pitfalls. The book is available from all good bookshops or direct from the publisher, How To Books (Tel: 01865 375794).

A superb property investment resource is also available on the world wide web. **PropertySecrets.net** offers its members advance notification of investment opportunities both in the UK and worldwide and provides a huge range of valuable information contained in regular bulletins, weekly newsletters and through an archive of constantly updated articles.

It is prudent to note that the Office of Fair Trading has recently campaigned for a greater public awareness of 'property investment scams' operating in the UK. These advertised 'get rich quick' schemes target novice property investors with unbeatable deals and make promises that 'you too can become a millionaire'. Most of the schemes produce poor results and some are simply fraudulent. Remember one simple thing ... if these people are millionaires, why are they explaining their secrets to you? The answer is usually that they *take your money* and *give nothing* of any value in return. Beware all such schemes and **never** hand over your hard-earned cash to anyone promoting unsubstantiated claims of wealth.

The BBC recently reported on some of the more typical scams:

> Investors attend a free presentation, which aims to persuade them to hand over large amounts of money to enrol on a course promising to make them a successful property dealer. Schemes can involve the offer of buying yet-to-be-built properties at a discount. Other variations include a buy-to-let scheme where companies offer to source, renovate and manage properties, claiming good returns from rental income. The properties are generally near-derelict and the tenants non-existent.

For more information, visit the OFT site: **www.oft.gov.uk/Consumer/Scams**

An inherited property

Acquiring an inheritance in the form of property can be advantageous, but only if it conforms to all the criteria for letting so far outlined. There is little point in having a golden chalice if there is no fitting use for it. The property may be in the wrong location or lack appropriate qualities for letting. Consider the merits of selling it to finance a more suitable acquisition elsewhere. Bear in mind that selling will involve additional costs and potential liability for capital gains tax. Consult your accountant before taking action as the timing of a sale and subsequent purchase can influence the degree of liability.

TIMING IS EVERYTHING!

Time really *does* cost money, and this is no more certain than in the period from receiving the keys for your property to having tenants occupying it. Make every attempt to reduce lost income by manipulating the completion date to fall in line with your plans. If repairs are needed make certain that your contractors are *ready to go*; have decorators on stand-by; have furnishings and appliances identified and have adequate funds available to purchase them.

If possible, arrange for completion to occur during good letting months and **not** just before Christmas or during very cold and wet periods. Undertake as much as possible in advance so that once you have the keys you can get the property earning money for you.

SUMMARY

- Assess each property carefully before you purchase. Calculate and compare running costs and the forecasted yield to identify the best buy.
- Be aware of how your tax liability will influence profit.
- Inspect the building's fabric and arrange a survey so that defects and repair costs can be properly evaluated.
- Research the best method of funding your investment. Use the internet and/or a mortgage broker to find the best deal available. Before accepting a mortgage, check that letting is permitted and identify any associated charges or mandatory procedures.
- Organise as much as possible ahead of purchase to prevent losing income through having an empty dwelling.

CHAPTER THREE

Legally Required
Pre-Letting Inspections

In this chapter:

- how the law will affect you
- electrical safety legislation
- gas safety legislation
- furnishings legislation
- fire safety legislation
- health and safety issues.

HOW THE LAW WILL AFFECT YOU

Landlords in England and Wales must comply with a large volume of legislation. Failure to do so can lead to severe fines and even imprisonment. Some landlords flout the law foolishly believing they will not get caught; others do so out of ignorance. Either way, they run the risk of losing their entire business and, where culpable injury has occurred, their freedom too.

To comply with current Regulations, the following inspections *must* be conducted *before* a property is tenanted.

ELECTRICAL SAFETY LEGISLATION

Although there is no statutory requirement to have rented property formally inspected for electrical safety at set periods, landlords are legally required to provide a dwelling that is safe. The laws affecting them include:

- The Electrical Equipment (Safety) Regulations 1994
- The Plugs and Sockets (Safety) Regulations 1994
- The Consumer Protection Act 1987
- The Low Voltage Electrical Equipment Regulations 1989
- The General Product Safety Regulations 1994
- The Health and Safety at Work Act 1974 (this Act inflicts an implied liability on letting agents and those who gain from self-employment, as is the case with most landlords).

25

Some of these regulations only affect letting agents and those who rent property commercially or for business. There is debate about whether individual landlords letting a single dwelling without an agent must comply with all of them. However, as failing to comply can result in fines of up to £5,000 per offence, up to six months' imprisonment, being sued by the tenant for civil damages and, in the event of a death occurring, possible manslaughter charges, it is better to observe them and feel confident about your letting.

In January 2005 new legislation made it a legal requirement, under Part P of the Building Regulations, for certain types of electrical work in dwellings and associated buildings such as garages, sheds, greenhouses and outbuildings, to comply with relevant standards. In short, the change means that anyone conducting certain 'notifiable' types of electrical work, including some tasks that previously might have been thought of as do-it-yourself work, must either be registered with one of the government approved Competent Person Self-Certification Schemes or they must submit a building notice to the local authority before starting the work. For further guidance contact the National Inspection Council for Electrical Installation Contracting (NICEIC) by telephone on 01582 531000 or visit their website at **www.niceic.org.uk**

A wise landlord will employ a qualified electrician for an initial and further periodic inspections, producing a test report which can later be attached to the inventory. Ideally, the inspection should be carried out prior to each tenancy commencing, or at least annually. To become compliant, the following are recommended:

◆ Check that all appliance manuals, instructions, safety notices and labels are available so that copies can be issued to tenants.
◆ Have a qualified electrician check that all appliances are safely wired and operate properly.
◆ Do not buy second-hand electrical goods unless you can prove they are safe and have the appropriate instructions.
◆ Check that appliances have no damaged, worn or loose cables and that plugs are securely fitted and properly fused.
◆ Check that plugs and sockets conform to BS1363 or BS1363/A.
◆ Make certain that appropriate appliances are earthed.
◆ Have a qualified electrician inspect the property wiring (power and lighting), earthing, sockets, switches and fusing system, to ensure they meet current regulations and operate properly.
◆ Remember to inspect *all* areas of the property, including any attic or loft space, garage, outbuilding, shed and garden, and any appliances in them.

Copies of these and other Regulations can be obtained from The Stationery Office (TSO), telephone customer services on 0870 600 5522 for details or view them online at **www.opsi.gov.uk**

GAS SAFETY LEGISLATION

The law affecting individual landlords with regard to gas safety is more absolute than for electrical safety. It includes:

◆ The Gas Safety (Installation and Use) Regulations 1998
◆ The Gas Cooking Appliances (Safety) Regulations 1989.

Part of the landlord's statutory duty involves arranging for an annual gas safety inspection by a CORGI (Council for Registered Gas Installers) registered engineer. Failure to comply is a criminal offence and a fine of up to £5,000 and/or six months' imprisonment can be imposed. In serious cases civil proceedings can also be brought against the landlord. The Regulations include requirements that a landlord must:

◆ Ensure there is no open-flue gas appliance in any bedroom or any room where people may sleep, a bathroom or shower-room.
◆ Ensure that any work to or installation of gas appliances, fittings or equipment is conducted by a CORGI registered installer.
◆ Ensure that both fixed and mobile gas appliances and associated pipes and flues are safely maintained and that a formal safety inspection is conducted at least once a year by a CORGI registered installer.
◆ Ensure that, following any work to any gas appliance, a CORGI registered engineer conducts a defined series of tests to guarantee safety.
◆ Give tenants access to all appropriate manuals, safety notices and labels, and all instructions, for any gas appliance supplied.
◆ Keep adequate records of gas appliances including the dates of formal inspections and details of any defects identified and work required or conducted. A copy of the records must be made available to the tenant within 28 days of the inspection or prior to occupation if it is a new tenancy.
◆ Keep safety inspection reports and certificates issued by a CORGI installer for a minimum of two years.
◆ Prevent tenants from using any gas appliance where its safety or proper installation is suspect or a fault known.

In addition, landlords are advised to make tenants fully aware of *their* obligations under the Regulations which include:

◆ They must not interfere with, add to or otherwise conduct any work on any gas appliance, installation or associated pipes.

- They must inform the landlord immediately if they suspect a fault.
- They must take appropriate emergency action according to the situation. If they smell gas or suspect an appliance or installation to be dangerous, they should turn the gas supply off at the main cut-off valve and inform The National Grid on emergency telephone number 0800 111999. The National Grid own, operate and develop the high-voltage electricity transmission network in England and Wales and Great Britain's principal natural gas transportation system.
- They should provide access to the property, given reasonable notice in writing, for the landlord's engineer to conduct the annual gas safety inspection.
- They should not introduce to the property any mobile or fixed gas appliance known or suspected to be faulty.

When arranging for a gas safety inspection, ask the engineer for a CORGI identification-card number and registration number. To verify the authenticity of their registration, call CORGI on 0800 915 0485 or visit the internet website at **www.trustcorgi.com** Visitors to the site can also locate an engineer in their area. Copies of the Gas Safety (Installation and Use) Regulations 1998 can be obtained from The Stationery Office (TSO), telephone customer services on 0870 600 5522 for details or view them online at **www.opsi.gov.uk**

Landlords should consider offering their tenants a defence against the potentially fatal consequences of carbon-monoxide (CO) poisoning. CO is produced through inadequate combustion of solid, gas or liquid fuels, usually due to faulty or badly installed appliances and blocked or damaged flues. Installing a carbon-monoxide alarm provides an effective early-warning system. Units can be bought for about £30 from good DIY stores.

FURNISHINGS LEGISLATION

Landlords must ensure that furnishings meet the standards enforced under current regulations. The effective legislation includes:

- The Furniture and Furnishings (Fire) (Safety) Regulations 1988 (amended in 1989 and 1993)
- The Consumer Protection Act 1987.

Some professionals question whether an individual landlord letting a property on a one-off short-term basis, and not as part of a business, needs to comply with these Regulations. Interpretation of the law is a matter for the courts; however, landlords must consider the repercussions of failing to comply. The penalties include a fine of £5,000 per item not complying and/or six months' imprisonment. The consequences resulting from injury or death of a tenant are much more serious. Remember that, unless you receive professional legal advice before letting the property, your liability status may at best be precarious. Novice landlords should therefore err on the side of caution by verifying that furnishings comply. The Regulations were brought into force following numerous deaths caused by fire and smoke inhalation from foam-filled and other furnishings. Manufacturers are legally bound to produce safe products and all furnishings purchased new should comply with the minimum legal requirements. This fact does not, however, offer a landlord any degree of certainty in complying.

A landlord must supply only approved goods and have evidence that the appropriate labels are affixed to them. Examples of display labels and permanent labels are shown in Figures 3 and 4; the Regulations contain full-size colour illustrations. Landlords must examine the actual Regulations for reference purposes.

Items that must comply include:

- three-piece suites, armchairs and sofas
- futons, bed settees and other 'convertible' furnishings
- beds and bed bases as well as mattresses, headboards and pillows
- cushions and fitted or loose seating, pillows and pads
- stretch, loose and fitted covers for furniture
- dining and kitchen chairs with upholstered seats, backs or arms
- nursery furniture including baby chairs, cots and changing mats
- garden furniture containing upholstery that might be used indoors.

Specifically excluded are:

- carpets
- curtains
- loose mattress covers
- pillow cases
- sleeping bags
- antique furniture or furniture manufactured prior to 1950 (you may be required to provide the Trading Standards Office with evidence of the manufactured date or a statement of age given by an appropriately experienced assessor)
- bed clothes (including duvets).

Upholstered furnishing must have fire resistant filling and pass the 'match' and 'cigarette' test to be compliant with the Regulations. They must also have affixed to them the appropriate manufacturer's label (see Figure 4). Beds and mattresses do not need to have permanent labels attached but must meet British Standard BS7177 (a label attached at purchase should confirm this).

Filling material(s) and covering
fabric(s) meet the requirements
for resistance to cigarette and
match ignition in
the 1988 safety regulations

**CARELESSNESS
CAUSES FIRE**

Fig. 3. Example of a furniture display label.

CARELESSNESS
CAUSES FIRE

A N Other Ltd. AB1 2XY

AB 1234

1 March 1990

**This article contains CM Foam
which passes the specified test.
All upholstery is cigarette resistant.**

All cover fabric is cotton and is match resistant.

This article does not include a include a
Schedule 3 interliner. rliner.

Fig. 4. Example of a permanent furniture label.

Labels can get damaged or become loose or worn over time and, as these are your main evidence proving compliance, you should record details at the point of purchase. Register:

◆ the date of purchase
◆ where purchased
◆ the manufacturer
◆ model and reference numbers
◆ a verbatim transcript of what is displayed on any label(s).

Pin to this record your purchase receipt and a photograph of the item of furnishing with the permanent label(s) clearly visible. Keep these in a safe place for future reference. The Department of Trade and Industry has produced a useful free Guide to the Furniture and Furnishings (Fire) (Safety) Regulations which includes a pictorial reference of all mandatory labels required. Contact the Department's Publications Unit on 0845 015 0010 or visit **www.dti.gov.uk/ccp/topics1/guide/furnitureguide.pdf** for an online printable version. A copy of the full regulations can be obtained from The Stationery Office (TSO), telephone customer services on 0870 600 5522 for details or view online at **www.opsi.gov.uk**

FIRE SAFETY LEGISLATION

The relevant legislation includes:

◆ The General Product Safety Regulations 1994
◆ The Housing (Management of Houses in Multiple Occupation) Regulations 1990
◆ Fire Precautions Act 1971 (S.10)
◆ Housing Acts 1980 and 1985
◆ The Consumer Protection Act 1987

Some of these Acts and Regulations apply only to HiMO landlords and/or commercial landlords who let property as part of a business. Current legislation does, however, provide various powers to local authorities, trading standards officers, environmental health officers, the fire service, and/or other agencies, to inspect properties reported or suspected to be unsafe. All landlords should examine their property and the appliances and furnishings therein to ensure they meet the required standards. In particular:

◆ Communal hallways and staircases should be free of any obstructions which may inhibit a quick exit during a fire. Carpet laid to stair-steps must be secure with no threadbare patches that could cause someone to trip or fall.

◆ If extinguishers and other fire-fighting equipment are provided, they should be in good working order and meet the required British Standard. User instructions should be easy to read and the equipment should be tested according to the manufacturer's guide or appropriate legislation, depending on the type of property being let (consult your local environmental health department).

◆ Properties considered to be a HiMO (see Chapter 1) must conform to the fire-safety standards enforced by the local authority.

◆ Consider the fire escape route and assess whether it could be improved.

◆ If you are considering making significant changes to the dwelling, be certain to check with the local authority planning department/building control before proceeding, to ensure compliance with building and fire safety regulations.

◆ Building Regulations require all properties built after June 1992 to have a mains powered inter-connected smoke-alarm system installed. Landlords of older properties should consider providing at least a battery-operated smoke-detector as it will add considerably to the safety of their tenants. Alarms should be fitted in an effective location and supplied with new batteries at the start of each tenancy. Testing and maintenance should be specified within the tenancy agreement, so that all are clearly aware of who is responsible.

HEALTH AND SAFETY ISSUES

By supplying accommodation, furnishings, appliances and equipment to tenants, you are required by law to observe the health and safety issues that may affect them. The laws and regulations previously mentioned in this chapter apply, as do the following additions with regard to health and safety:

◆ Landlord and Tenant Act 1985
◆ Defective Premises Act 1972
◆ Environmental Protection Act 1990

The implications of these Acts mean you must conduct a risk assessment of the property you intend letting and satisfy yourself that the property and its contents are safe. The Housing Act 2004 introduced a new 'Housing Health and Safety Rating System' (HHSRS), which became effective in April 2006. The new system does not negate the landlord's repairing obligations under the Landlord and Tenant Act 1985, which continues to apply. HHSRS provides local authorities with new powers and responsibilities to inspect properties reported as being unsafe and then take appropriate action against the landlord/owner. HHSRS replaces the prior fitness test for houses in multiple occupation (HiMO) contained within the Housing Act 1985. The new measures apply to **all** dwellings, not just to HiMOs or properties that are rented though they will mainly impact on HiMO landlords seeking a licence to operate. Local authorities will inspect properties under 29 categories of housing hazard. These are:

Physiological
- Damp and mould growth
- Cold
- Heat
- Asbestos and man made fibres
- Biocides
- Carbon monoxide
- Lead
- Radiation
- Uncombusted fuel
- Volatile organic compounds

Psychological
- Crowding and space
- Entry by intruders
- Lighting
- Noise

Infection
- Domestic hygiene etc.
- Food safety
- Personal hygiene
- Water supply

Safety
- Falls in baths etc.
- Falls on the level
- Falls on stairs etc.
- Falls from windows etc.
- Electrical hazards
- Fire hazards
- Hot surfaces etc.
- Collision/entrapment
- Ergonomics
- Explosions
- Structural collapse

For most non-HiMO landlords, the following represent the more likely and significant areas of health and safety concern:

Asbestos

Does the property contain asbestos? Older properties were often built using asbestos for sewerage pipes, drainage, roofing and to line walls. Removal is usually required unless it is in good order and safely encapsulated. Consult the local environmental health department for further advice.

Damp and mould

High levels of humidity, combined with inadequate ventilation, is a serious health hazard for occupiers. Any condensation or dampness should be investigated and the cause remedied.

Ventilation

Unventilated bathrooms and kitchens should have a ceiling or wall-mounted extractor fan. Opening windows should be tested after any painting has been undertaken.

Sharp objects

Examine the property for protruding nails, broken or cracked glass and any splintered timbers that may cause injury. Repair or replace as necessary before the property is occupied.

Sanitation

Basins, sinks, baths, shower bases, toilet bowls and cisterns should be free of defects. Any that are cracked or damaged should be replaced.

Safety rails

The bannister rails leading up a staircase must be securely fixed, as should bath-handles (where fitted), any rails leading down into a cellar, and any gallery or balcony railings.

Carpets

Floor coverings should always be in a good condition with no threadbare, loose or worn areas that could cause an accident. It is impossible for all eventualities to be considered and the law recognises that tenants must employ a degree of commonsense when occupying a property. However, landlords have a **duty of care** to their tenants and must take all necessary precautions to supply safe accommodation, free of any obvious hazard.

SUMMARY

♦ As a landlord letting property in England and Wales, you must comply with the laws and regulations affecting you and your property

♦ Arrange for both electrical and gas safety inspections to be conducted in accordance with the appropriate legislation and before occupation of the property by tenants.

♦ Inspect all furnishings and confirm that they comply with the Furniture and Furnishings (Fire) (Safety) Regulations 1988 (as amended in 1989 and 1993). Resist the temptation to buy second-hand goods if compliance is suspect or cannot be proved.

♦ Be aware of the fire-safety laws affecting your property and, if in any doubt about compliance, consult the environmental health officer of the local authority.

♦ Inspect for any potentially hazardous installations, fittings, equipment or appliances that could lead to injury or ill-health. Repair or replace anything that is damaged, cracked, loose or otherwise defective.

CHAPTER FOUR

Preparing the Property for Tenants

In this chapter:

- decoration
- furnished or unfurnished?
- insurance
- creating an introductory pack
- manuals, keys and code numbers.

Good preparation from the start will mean fewer problems later. These are the final tasks you need to perform before introducing viewers to the dwelling.

DECORATION

No matter how careful your tenant is, there will always be minor damage to décor. Use materials that are easily renewed; paint is the obvious first choice as it is inexpensive and quick to apply. As a general guide consider the following:

- Don't use strong exotic colours; not all potential tenants will find them attractive. Instead, use matt emulsion off-white shades or magnolia for all walls. This creates an illusion of space and will appeal to most people.
- Retain a small amount of paint to repair minor scuff marks caused during tenancy.
- Paint all skirtings, timber window frames and sills, doors and door frames with white gloss.
- Paint ceilings with a proprietary matt white emulsion.

FURNISHED OR UNFURNISHED?

Local demand will be a major influence in deciding whether to furnish your property. Where there is a highly mobile tenant population, for example within large inner city areas, it is often better to offer a furnished dwelling. This group move frequently and usually do not want the added cost and inconvenience of transporting their possessions.

Conversely, in some rural areas with a less mobile population and where tenancy terms are longer, it can be worth offering a property unfurnished. These tenants often want to establish a home and will wish to fill it with possessions of their own choice and style.

Consider the following when making your decision.

The disadvantages of supplying furnished

♦ The landlord is liable for the repair or replacement of any furniture, appliances and equipment supplied during the tenancy (subject to the tenancy agreement wording and statutory rights of the tenant).

♦ Any furniture, appliances and equipment must be supplied in a good and safe condition and some items must be professionally inspected (see Chapter 3).

♦ Your choice of furnishings may discourage some would-be tenants whose personal preference and style may differ.

♦ The cost of supplying, maintaining and replacing furnishings may not be offset by a higher rent, particularly with larger properties where a vast array of items will be required.

♦ Between tenancies, furnishings and equipment will be vulnerable to theft or accidental damage. Landlords should consider arranging suitable insurance cover to protect them.

♦ Dwellings that are unfurnished **and** unoccupied are usually exempt from council tax for the first six months, then landlords are liable to pay a 50 per cent rate until the property is reoccupied. Recent changes introduced now allow local authorities to use their discretion in deciding whether to apply the discounted rate to second homes and let property.

♦ Creating an inventory of furnishings, appliances and equipment at the start of tenancy, and checking it again at the end, takes time. The more items there are on the inventory, the longer it will take. If an inventory clerk is employed, the cost will be an additional expense deducted from rental income.

The advantages of supplying furnished

♦ A furnished dwelling can appear more homely and be more appealing to would-be tenants. This may result in faster occupation rates and reduced void periods.

♦ Less damage will be caused to walls and doors because tenants will not have to move large items in and out.

♦ Supplying furnishings can be expensive to people with restricted finance. Although the rent may be a fraction higher in comparison with an unfurnished dwelling, it may seem advantageous to the tenant to have them provided, with the cost extended over a long period.

♦ HM Revenue & Customs provide landlords of furnished properties with an allowance against tax currently at 10 per cent of the rent to cover depreciation, repair and replacement.

If, after careful consideration, you decide to let your property furnished, only provide the essentials. Remember you are not supplying a holiday letting – so don't provide small, inconsequential items such as cutlery, pictures, pots and pans, ornaments and linen. Most tenants will wish to acquire these themselves to create a home characterised by their own personality and taste.

Don't supply hi-tech equipment such as a video, television or hi-fi unit. These are vulnerable items if left in an unoccupied property. They are also expensive to repair or replace. Note also that landlords who provide a television are liable for the licence fee during empty periods.

INSURANCE

Although you may already have either buildings and/or contents insurance for your property, there are good reasons for carefully assessing the protection they provide. Many policies offer no cover for tenanted properties, whilst others do not offer sufficient protection. Some only do so for certain types of tenant. Read the small print thoroughly and assess their value based on the letting plans you have made. Consider in each case whether the policy includes:

◆ Loss of rent if the property becomes uninhabitable.
◆ The expense of providing suitable alternative accommodation if the tenant has to temporarily move out for repairs and where the cost is greater than the rent currently being paid.
◆ Cover regardless of the tenant type (some policies prohibit students and/or tenants in receipt of benefit).
◆ Cover during empty periods.
◆ Accidental damage to the landlord's possessions (there is no statutory requirement to insure the tenant's possessions, though in some circumstances they may have grounds to seek compensation).
◆ Public liability cover where a tenant, their guest or other visitor injures themselves due to a fault in the building or any supplied furniture or equipment.
◆ Legal expenses cover should a tenant decide to take court proceedings against you.

Some insurance policies are specifically designed for let-property. Although many are only available through letting agents, some landlords' associations also provide them, and the cost of membership can often be fully reimbursed through reduced insurance premiums. Check *Yellow Pages* or consult your local authority for any groups that have been established in your local area. Searching for cost-effective landlord/rented property insurance can be a nightmare, because there are so many variables involved. Try visiting **www.landlordzone.co.uk** and click the 'insurance' link for useful additional information and recommended brokers/insurers.

CREATING AN INTRODUCTORY PACK

There is no legal obligation to provide tenants with an introductory pack, but it *is* advisable. Anything that assists them to enjoy the property and its location may encourage a renewal of tenancy. In addition, providing instructions may prevent accidental damage occurring as tenants try to operate equipment using guesswork alone. A comprehensive pack might include:

◆ Instructions and/or operation manuals for all supplied equipment, appliances, systems and installations.
◆ Information about security matters including contact details for the local police and any Neighbourhood Watch scheme.
◆ Your contact details, including any out-of-hours emergency telephone number.
◆ A local map.
◆ Bus and train timetables.
◆ Guide notes for cleaning the oven, freezer, curtains and carpets.
◆ Emergency telephone numbers for gas, water and electricity.
◆ Information on local schools, libraries, leisure facilities, good bars and recommended restaurants, the nearest park, train station, bus stop, etc.
◆ Information about where the mains water stop-tap is located.
◆ Information about where the electricity and gas meters are located together with guide notes on how to turn off each supply.
◆ Space for copies of the tenancy agreement, inventory and any letters you send to the tenants.

The pack can be used for each subsequent tenancy, expanding with additional information as required. A wallet-file with A4 document pockets will help keep everything organised.

MANUALS, KEYS AND CODE NUMBERS
Manuals

Legislation demands that landlords supply instruction manuals or written guide notes for certain types of equipment, appliances, installations and systems. It is good practice to give tenants a *full* range of instructions for all the goods provided. Unfortunately, tenants have a habit of losing these documents, so give copies and keep the originals safe.

Copy keys

Landlords should have one set of keys for each tenant plus two sets for themselves. This may seem excessive, but if a tenant loses their keys and demands a new set on Sunday afternoon, obtaining new copies from the master set could prove difficult. Always imagine the worst-case scenario . . . and then have a plan to deal with it!

You will need copies of *all* keys, not just those for the main entrance door. This might include a garage, garden shed, conservatory, patio doors, window locks, garden gate, any padlocks supplied, mail-box or outhouse.

Code numbers

Some alarm systems, communal entrance doors and security gates use a code number. It is imperative that your tenants are issued with these codes but a security risk might arise when the tenant finally vacates. To combat this, never supply an instruction manual that includes a procedure for changing the code. Instead, obliterate this section when copying the manual so that you alone have access to this process. When the tenant vacates, the code can be altered, and security will be maintained.

SUMMARY

◆ Use paint, not wallpaper, when decorating as it is easier to maintain and renew.
◆ Decide whether or not to furnish your property according to the local demand. Supply only essential and bulky items, and of a quality and style appropriate for the type of tenant.
◆ Check that existing insurance policies adequately protect you and your property. Confirm that letting is not prohibited. Assess the value of changing your policies to ones specifically designed for landlords.
◆ Create an introductory pack for your tenants and include copies of all manuals and instructions for equipment, appliances and systems.
◆ Ensure you have enough copy keys.
◆ Maintain security when issuing tenants with code numbers.

CHAPTER FIVE

Creating an Inventory

In this chapter:

- identifying the inspection areas
- using a reference guide
- undertaking the inspection
- creating the inventory
- the value of photographs
- inventory clerks
- template forms.

An entire chapter has been dedicated to this subject ... and with good reason! The **inventory** of furnishings and fittings is one of the most important documents a landlord can create, yet so few do it properly. Many believe it is sufficient to list items haphazardly with little or no regard to accurate identification, description or condition. It is little wonder that these same landlords suffer the consequences of a protracted dispute at the end of tenancy, when damage is found and they claim compensation from the tenant's deposit.

The inventory is the landlord's only evidence of how the property was provided at the outset. It should accurately describe, in fine detail, everything within it. Should a damage claim disagreement have to be settled in court or through the formal tenancy deposit protection dispute resolution service, this document will need to paint a tangible picture to people who have not seen the accommodation, so that a judgment can be made. Time and care should be taken *now* to produce a comprehensive and faithful report that can be relied upon later, should the need arise.

IDENTIFYING THE INSPECTION AREAS

Start by walking through and around the property, listing every space within it. This will provide the headings you will use later to catalogue items in the spaces. Ensure these 'titles' are descriptive of the rooms to which they relate. Rather than use '*Bedroom No 1*', you might call it '*Largest Bedroom to Front Elevation*', which more accurately identifies its location within the dwelling. Include any loft-space or cellar, garden areas, shed, greenhouse, garage, staircase, landing, hallway, hot-water tank cupboard, storage cupboard, conservatory, vestibule, balcony, roof-terrace or patio. Now take as many sheets of paper as required and write one heading at the top of each.

Only include those areas pertinent to the tenancy. Exclusive possession cannot be granted to regions such as communal gardens or shared entrances and stairwells. These should therefore be excluded from the inventory.

USING A REFERENCE GUIDE

Before conducting an inspection, it is useful to have a reference to remind you of the various observations you need to make as you progress through each space within and around the property. On a separate sheet of paper, write the following:

1. **Colour**. Be descriptive. '*Post-box red*' is clearer than '*red*' alone.
2. **Material**. Cotton, wood, glass, metal, ceramic, etc. Be specific, but only if you are certain; use '*bronze figurine*' only if you are certain the material is bronze. An alternative might be '*dark metal figurine*'.
3. **Manufacturer**. Who produced it? Most goods are labelled or stamped with the manufacturer's name.
4. **Model/serial number or name**. As 3 above.
5. **Size**. Be as precise as possible. Use a ruler or tape measure.
6. **Shape**. Is it square, oval, spherical, box, etc?
7. **Labels**. This is to remind you to check the existence of a compliance label on furnishings requiring one (see Chapter 3). Make a note identifying the location of any fixed labels, for example '*under seat cushion*'.
8. **Condition**. Look for cracks, stains, blemishes, marks, scratches, scuffs, erosion, fading or wearing. Carefully detail the degree and location of any damage. Decide whether the item is in **good** (as new), **fair** or **poor** condition.
9. **Tested**. What date was the item last tested (electrical and/or gas appliances, equipment, installations and systems)? Refer to the engineer's report.

UNDERTAKING THE INSPECTION

You will need:

♦ the reference guide
♦ headed sheets
♦ tape measure
♦ step-ladders for access into the loft, if necessary.

Start at the uppermost part of the property. It is important that nothing is missed from the inventory so be logical in your approach. Examine the ceiling and any light fittings. Then work down each wall looking at the windows, any curtains or blinds, pictures, shelving and wall-heaters; end with the floor-covering and anything standing on it. Remember to include doors and skirtings, power-sockets, wall-coverings, and any items stored in cupboards.

Once the interior has been fully recorded, move outside (if appropriate) and examine the entrance doors, any porch, garden areas, sheds, greenhouse, garage, dividing wall or fence.

CREATING THE INVENTORY

Figure 5 is an example of how to compile the information into a single report. It describes part of one room only; it is not the entire inventory. Use this as a template for each room or space in your property, giving regard to any necessary alterations according to the design, size and quality of the dwelling and items it contains. At the top of each page write the address of the dwelling and the page number. At the bottom write '*Tenant(s) Signature(s)*' (tenants should always sign every page to prove they have seen them).

The bulk of the inventory is now complete. There are a few additions to be made, including a front page title:

INVENTORY and SCHEDULE OF CONDITION
of Furnishings and Fixtures for
(address of property to be tenanted)

The next page details '*Notes for the Tenant*'. These might include the following (but confirm that they are compatible with the wording of terms in the tenancy agreement, otherwise a conflict may arise):

- This inventory is an accurate description of items supplied with this property. It is agreed all items are in a good condition unless otherwise stated.
- The property is in a clean condition. Charges will be incurred by the tenant if, at the end of the tenancy, the property is returned in an inferior condition.
- All items of furnishing/appliances must be in their original location and position prior to vacating the property.
- Garden areas (if appropriate) must be returned at the end of tenancy in the same neat and well-maintained state.
- Carpets, curtains and other soft furnishings must be returned at the end of tenancy in the same condition as detailed in this inventory. There will be a charge for any stains, marks or other damage caused, according to the degree of reinstatement required.

PROPERTY ADDRESS:			Page No.
603 LAPWING COURT, JERRADNE WAY MANCHESTER M49 8URF.			**5** (KITCHEN)

QTY.	ITEM	DESCRIPTION	TENANT COMMENTS
	CEILING	WHITE PAINTED PLASTER IN GOOD CONDITION	
	WALLS	MAGNOLIA EMULSION PAINTED PLASTER IN A GOOD CONDITION	
	WINDOWS	x 2 UPVC DOUBLE GLAZED UNITS WITH CLEAR PANES IN GOOD CONDITION	
	FLOOR	VINYL TILED IN A PLAIN CREAM COLOUR GOOD CONDITION	
	TIMBERS INCLUDING DOOR, SKIRTINGS AND DOOR FRAME	PAINTED WHITE GLOSS, ALL IN A GOOD CONDITION	
1	CEILING MOUNTED FLORESCENT LIGHT FITTING	WITH DIFFUSER AND WORKING TUBE	
	RANGE OF FITTED MATCHING WALL AND BASE UNITS	WITH LIGHT NATURAL TIMBER DOORS AND DRAWER FRONTS WITH POLISHED METAL HANDLES ALL IN GOOD CONDITION	
	MOTTLED CREAM LAMINATE WORKTOPS	SCRATCH MARKS TO SURFACE NEAR SINK	
1	ZANUSSI AUTO WASHING MACHINE, PLUMBED IN, MODEL AQUACYCLE	SERIAL NO ZN335603F CLEAN CONDITION LAST SAFETY TEST UNDERTAKEN 23 FEB 2003	
1	WALL MOUNTED ELECTRIC STORAGE HEATER	SCRATCH TO PAINTED FRONT SURFACE LAST SAFETY TEST UNDERTAKEN ON 23 FEB 2003	
4	TIMBER FRAMED CHAIRS WITH UPHOLSTERED SEATS	BLUE AND WHITE STRIPE FABRIC FIRE SAFETY COMPLIANCE LABELS ATTACHED UNDER EACH SEAT. ONE SEAT STAINED.	

TENANT(S) SIGNATURE(S) ....

Fig. 5. Example page from an inventory.

- Fair wear and tear will be taken into consideration. However, you will be charged for damage to wallpaper, walls, doors, ceilings, and any other surface found punctured, scratched or otherwise damaged by nails, pins, hooks, screws, drills, knives or any other object.
- Breakages or damage must be reported and resolved at the time of occurrence and in a manner and quality commensurate with the item supplied.
- There must be no work, alteration or repair of any kind conducted to the structure of the property or to anything contained within it or to the grounds, unless the landlord's written authority has been received.
- Tenants must not, under any circumstances, change or add to any locking device within the property. All keys must be returned at the end of tenancy. If access cannot be gained by the landlord due to changed locks or missing keys, the tenant will be charged for any work or materials required.

The last page of the inventory should include any items not stored in any specific room. These might include:

- Appliance manuals – listed individually.
- Other instructions or care notices.
- The information pack.
- Keys – detail the number and type and the doors or windows they open.

This page should also include a space at the bottom for the tenant's name, his signature, the landlord's signature, the date, and a disclaiming statement similar to the following:

This inventory provides a detailed and fair account of the items provided to the tenant(s) on [date] and the condition of these items and of the décor, gardens (if any), fabrics, timbers, painted surfaces, and all other parts and objects forming the whole of the tenanted premises. The writer is not a surveyor, engineer or structural surveyor; nor is he an expert in materials, timbers, fabrics, colours, antiques, etc. Descriptions given are done so in good faith and with relevance only to their existence and perceived condition.

Two identical copies of the inventory will be required for 'check-in' (see Chapter 9).

Avoid the use of abbreviations

Do not use abbreviations unless a clear explanation of their meaning is given. Even the common use of 'N/A' for not applicable or 'WC' for water closet can lead to misinterpretation.

THE VALUE OF PHOTOGRAPHS

Photographic evidence of the condition of the property and its contents is an advantage. It will support the written inventory and graphically depict elements to any third party. When obtaining photographs:

- Take at least two or three wide shots in each room or area, paying particular attention to wall-coverings, carpets and the flat surfaces of tables.
- Capture specific items that may be prone to damage or which are of particular concern.
- Obtain evidence of a clean oven, hob, fridge, kitchen cupboards, shower or bath.
- If gardens are in a neat and well-maintained state, take a few photographs of the exterior.
- Use a camera that records the date on photographs. Alternatively, write the date pictures are taken on the reverse of photographs later.
- Use a video camera in preference, or in addition, to producing stills.

INVENTORY CLERKS

There are firms of inventory clerks who offer services to landlords for a fee. The main benefit is that a professional inventory is more likely to be considered impartial by all parties involved. This can be important if a dispute over dilapidations arises at the end of the tenancy. An experienced inventory clerk will differentiate fairly between wear and tear and damage; whereas a landlord could be biased in making judgement.

To locate a firm in your area consult *Yellow Pages* or telephone the *Association of Independent Inventory Clerks* on 01276 855388 or visit their website at **www.aiic.uk.com**

TEMPLATE FORMS

Inventory forms can be ordered at **www.lawpack.co.uk** at £4.49 each. These have not been examined by the author of this book and therefore no comment about quality or suitability can be given. A free version of an inventory form is also available online at **www.landlordzone.co.uk**

SUMMARY

- Identify the property's interior and exterior spaces and convert them into headings for the inventory.
- Create a reference of inspection elements.

- Undertake thorough scrutiny of the property contents and assess the condition of each item. Record full details including any identification model or serial numbers, manufacturer (if known), colour, shape and size.
- Record when electrical and gas appliances/fittings were last inspected for safety.
- Identify all fire safety labels and record where they are located if affixed to upholstered items.
- Create two copies of the inventory document. Ensure there is enough space for tenants to write their comments on the day of entry.
- Take photographs of the property interior and exterior.
- Consider employing an inventory clerk.

CHAPTER SIX

Finding Suitable Tenants

In this chapter:

- advertising the property
- the value of 'To Let' boards
- accepting pets and young children
- contacting local employers
- alternative tenant sources
- creating an application form
- showing the property
- interviewing potential tenants.

Finding a tenant is not difficult, but finding the *right* tenant is an entirely different matter. This chapter deals only with the initial part of this process; the next chapter looks at verifying the proposed tenant's identity and background.

ADVERTISING THE PROPERTY

Traditional advertising in local newspapers can produce a horde of enquiries, but can be expensive and not always successful. For the best results:

- Examine other landlords' advertisements and make your rent competitive, given the size and quality of accommodation and its location.
- Identify which editions of a daily newspaper are popular with those searching for let property.
- Use the three best assets of the dwelling in the first sentence of your advert.
- Plan ahead. Be available to answer calls once the advert is published. Avoid using an answer-machine as some callers will not leave a message.
- Be prepared. When calls are expected, have a couple of pens available (in case one fails), a notepad, calendar or diary for viewing appointments, and a list of suitable questions. Double-check that you have written down the enquirer's name, address and contact number accurately.

THE VALUE OF 'TO LET' BOARDS

'To Let' boards are of paramount importance, particularly where there are other dwellings to rent in the same area. Letting agents will be advertising these other properties and will attract and deliver interested potential tenants right to your doorstep. A 'To Let' board shows that you also have accommodation available and people will contact you for more information. Boards also inform neighbours who, in turn, will tell their friends, colleagues and relatives about the property. Do not underestimate the power of word-of-mouth.

Boards can be self-made or created professionally. Once tenants have been found, the board should be stored away so it can be used again when the property becomes vacant.

'To Let' boards are also available over the internet. As an example, **www.elmleaf.co.uk** offer two types of weather-resistant board starting at £32.95. Tel: 01943 430189.

The law states that 'To Let' signs must be removed within 14 days after tenants have been found. In 2006, five Cardiff agents were successfully prosecuted by council planners for the offence of causing visual detriment to a neighbourhood. Check the by-laws for your own local authority and any property leasehold restrictions that might apply, before erecting an exterior sign.

ACCEPTING PETS AND YOUNG CHILDREN

It is useful to decide whether or not you intend to accept tenancy applications from people with pets or young children. Determining this in advance greatly reduces the number of disappointed applicants but, by being selective, you will receive fewer enquiries.

Until the Office of Fair Trading (OFT) released its guidance notes on Unfair Terms in Tenancy Agreements in 2001 (which relate to the Unfair Terms in Consumer Contracts Regulations 1999), it was generally accepted that private sector landlords could prohibit the keeping of *all* pet animals through a clause in the tenancy agreement. This is no longer safe because the OFT considers it unfair when such a broad term prevents the tenant from keeping, for example, a goldfish. The guidance notes suggest that prohibiting a specific type of pet *that might harm the property or be a nuisance to other residents* would be more appropriate and less likely to meet the same objection.

However, once tenants are in occupation, it is unlikely that a landlord will regain possession through the courts simply because tenants have young children or are keeping pet animals. There would have to be considerable evidence of a nuisance to neighbours or excessive damage for there to be even a remote chance of success. Taking this into account, landlords should reject inappropriate tenants at the application stage.

CONTACTING LOCAL EMPLOYERS

Research shows that 75 per cent of people who drive to work live within two miles of their place of employment. The best way of targeting this group is to identify the major employing companies in the area and visit each one in person. Take with you a single page which describes the accommodation, the rent and your contact particulars. Make it more eye-catching by including a photograph. In addition:

◆ Take drawing-pins so that a copy can be attached to any staff notice board.

◆ Ask whether there is a company newsletter you can advertise in.

◆ Enquire about an *intranet* service where you can post your property details. An intranet is like the internet, but restricted to a company and its employees.

◆ Leave copies of the property details with any personnel or accommodation officer and explain that you would accept an individual tenancy or a company letting.

◆ Follow up your visits with courtesy telephone calls one week later to check for enquiries.

ALTERNATIVE TENANT SOURCES

There are scores of opportunities to advertise properties and find suitable tenants. These are just a few:

◆ Libraries often allow anyone to display information on public notice-boards.

◆ Most supermarkets have notice-boards for their customers to use.

◆ Colleges and universities often have information boards too. It is not only students who need accommodation but lecturers and administration staff as well.

◆ Hospitals are a good source for tenants. There are ancillary workers, administration staff, doctors and nurses always looking for rented property.

◆ Do not overlook local schools; teachers and other staff are often searching for homes nearby.

◆ Airports are also useful, particularly if you can find a notice-board inspected by flight-crew.

◆ Bus terminals and major railway stations often have hundreds of employees operating in and from them. Find the staff information board and pin details to it.

◆ If your property is an apartment, post copies of your details under each door in the block. Owners or tenants may have friends, colleagues or relatives looking for similar properties to rent.

◆ Although you may not wish to employ a managing agent, some letting agents offer a tenant-find-only service. The cost is usually about a month's rent equivalent.

The internet is a valuable source of advertising though success may be hit-and-miss because there are thousands of property related websites, each containing scores of property-to-let details; it must be like finding a needle in a haystack for tenants searching for a specific type of accommodation. The more popular websites charge a fee for advertising, but currently all of the following offer it free:

www.accommodation.com
www.ad-mart.co.uk
www.anyads.co.uk
www.easylet.org.uk
www.estateagent.co.uk
www.homes2rent.net
www.homesforstudents.co.uk
www.homeswithoutagents.com
www.let-a-property.info
www.letbynet.com

www.letsdirect.co.uk
www.lettingzone.com
www.loot.com
www.preloved.co.uk
www.propertylocator.co.uk
www.rentamatic.co.uk
www.rentmouse.com
www.residentialrentals.co.uk
www.simplyrent.co.uk
www.torent.co.uk

Two useful websites are available to landlords who specialise either in student accommodation or lettings to young professionals. These are:

www.accommodationforstudents.com and
www.accommodationforprofessionals.com

Whilst it is free to advertise on its own website, **www.homeswithoutagents.com** has an option for landlords to pay £19.99 to have their details appear on two of the UK's biggest property sites (PropertyFinder and AssertaHome).

To advertise on 150 of the most popular websites (prices start at £49.99 a month) including BTopenworld, Lycos, Fish4Homes, UpMyStreet and PropertyFinder, which collectively reach an estimated 2.5 million home-seekers, go to **www.houseladder.co.uk**

CREATING AN APPLICATION FORM

It is important to provide all potential tenants with an application form because:

◆ it ensures the collection of accurate personal data so that suitability can be properly assessed
◆ it provides the required information for referencing purposes

- it confirms the applicant's intention to proceed
- and it grants the landlord the authority to seek additional data from third parties (such as banks and employers).

Even more importantly:

- it can provide the landlord with a means of regaining possession through the courts using **Ground 17**. This relates to a tenancy based on information supplied by an applicant which is later found to be false or misleading.

The best application form is one devised to meet your own particular needs and circumstances. However, there are certain elements that are common to all landlords and all properties. These include:

1. The applicant's full name.
2. The applicant's full postal address, post-code and occupancy status (owner-occupier, tenant, lodger, parent's home, etc). Existing tenants should supply their landlord's contact details.
3. The applicant's prior address (if less than five years at the one above). As in 2 above, the status of residency should be identified.
4. The applicant's date of birth.
5. The full name(s) and age(s) of any person(s) intending to live with the applicant at the property. *Note*: a separate application form should be completed by each person over 18 proposing to be a joint-tenant, i.e. who intend paying rent and/or residing as a co-tenant.
6. The relationship of all named at 5 above to the applicant, for example, husband, wife, partner, parent, guardian, colleague, friend.
7. Occupation details including whether full-time, part-time or self-employed. The period with the current employer, salary (excluding bonuses, commissions and over-time), position held, and the full name, address and telephone number of the employer.
8. If not employed, the funds from which rent will be paid. This may be a pension, housing benefit, capital in bank, etc.
9. Details of previous or existing criminal convictions (Rehabilitation of Offenders Act) or County Court Judgements (CCJs). If none, it is important the applicant states so in writing.
10. Whether a pet will be kept in the dwelling and, if so, the type of pet.
11. Whether the applicant is a smoker.
12. Bank details including the name of the account (important with joint accounts if the second account holder needs to give permission for information to be released), the account number, sort-code, and name and address of the bank.
13. Accountant's details (if self-employed) plus a copy of the last year's annual accounts.

14. Whether the applicant has ever been declared bankrupt.
15. Character reference details.
16. The applicant's National Insurance number.
17. The name, address and relationship to any intended guarantor. If there is none arranged, then the applicant should confirm this.
18. Proof of identification. It is important to confirm the person applying for tenancy is the same person who views the property. Ask for copies of the applicant's passport *and* driving-licence *or* birth-certificate.

There should be a space for a signature on each page of the form. The final section should include a statement as follows (providing it is compatible with the wording of the tenancy agreement and does not create any confusion or conflict):

This application is for a residential Assured Shorthold tenancy at (address) for a period of (fixed term). I understand the rent payable will be £(amount) per month by bank standing-order. I understand and accept that I will be liable for payment of the council tax, all gas and electricity charges, water and sewerage charges, any telephone service, cable and satellite service charges and the television licence, during the period of tenancy. I will be responsible for opening accounts with service providers at the start of tenancy and for closing accounts and making final balance payments at the end of tenancy.

Upon entry to the property I will pay one month's rent in advance together with a security deposit of £(amount) in cash or bank-draft. The security deposit will be retained in lieu of any damage, breakages, cleaning, unpaid accounts and/or keys and locks needing replacement (other than normal fair wear and tear). I understand that the deposit cannot be used for rent payment during the tenancy.

I confirm that the information provided in this application is correct and accurate and I understand that applying for a tenancy does not create a tenancy agreement or contract.

I hereby authorise the landlord (or his agent) to release copies of this application to third parties, seek references and conduct credit and other personal and/or financial checks as required, within the confines of the Data Protection Act 1988.

This application is subject to contract and dependent upon the landlord's approval before presentation of a tenancy agreement will be considered. A tenancy will not be created until all applicants have signed a tenancy agreement.

Directly below the statement leave a space for the applicant's full name and signature and the date.

There are several versions of tenancy application forms freely available on the internet. One of the best can be found at **www.landlordzone.co.uk**

Before devising and issuing an application form to would-be tenants, read Chapter 7. There are important documents which need to be attached to it and circumstances regarding references which could affect the style of form created.

In addition, read Chapter 9 regarding tenancy deposits, because regulations contained within the Housing Act 2004 have been introduced, which restricts the right a landlord has to personally collect and hold on to tenant deposit funds. Any application form devised will need to reflect these amendments.

SHOWING THE PROPERTY

When undertaking viewings:

◆ Record full details of the people you meet including their full name, address and telephone number.

◆ Prepare a brief description of the accommodation, deposit and rent, which can be handed to viewers.

◆ Be aware of personal security issues. If undertaking the viewing on your own, inform a friend or relative of the appointment and arrange to telephone them at an agreed time afterwards.

◆ Maintain property security. Do not explain the operation of alarm systems or locking devices.

◆ Once the appointment is over, record a brief description of the viewers for future reference.

INTERVIEWING POTENTIAL TENANTS

This type of interview can be undertaken without the candidate ever knowing it. It is not a formal interview, but an assessment conducted surreptitiously, beginning with the first telephone conversation. The caller's main objective is to find out more about the property; yours is to find out more about the caller.

During this initial conversation you should be able to find out whether they intend living on their own or with a joint-tenant; whether married or single; age; telephone manner; whether they work; how long they intend living at the property; where they live now and why they are moving. At the viewing you can observe their punctuality, if smartly dressed and polite. Questions can be asked about employment, financial situation and current accommodation.

Once the viewing is over, write a short description and appraisal of the candidate for future reference. Make a note of your instinctive feelings ... did you like the individual? Did they seem honest, reliable and trustworthy? Intuition is no substitute for thorough referencing, but it can expose adverse characteristics an individual may be attempting to hide.

SUMMARY

◆ Take every opportunity to market the property to neighbours, colleagues and local employees through traditional advertising, using notice-boards and by erecting a 'To Let' board.

◆ Decide in advance whether to accept tenants with pets or young children, but be aware that it may not always be so easy to prohibit either once a tenancy has begun.

◆ Take advantage of free advertising on the internet.

◆ Create a tenant application form pertinent to your own property and requirements.

◆ Undertake viewings and record important details about potential tenants who show an interest.

CHAPTER SEVEN

Tenant Referencing

In this chapter:

- ◆ receiving and assessing applications
- ◆ discrimination
- ◆ employing a reference agency
- ◆ obtaining an employment reference
- ◆ obtaining a bank reference
- ◆ obtaining credit references
- ◆ obtaining a landlord's reference
- ◆ verifying the home address
- ◆ charging costs to the applicant
- ◆ guarantors
- ◆ company-let referencing.

Appearances can be very misleading. An applicant may seem perfectly suitable at the first meeting. They may be smartly dressed, courteous and respectful. They may appear financially secure and offer to pay the deposit and first month's rent in cash. They may provide credible information that adequately explains their reason for moving.

But this portrayal of the perfect tenant might be a charade. Some of the worst tenants around are adept in the art of deceit, often duping numerous landlords. They will attempt to manoeuvre you into providing them with a tenancy using feigned respect, the lure of cash payments and the promise of a long, trouble-free term of occupancy.

Referencing verifies that the applicant is who they say they are and have the means to pay the rent. Some landlords overlook this essential task and suffer the consequences of housing a bad tenant as a result. Referencing does not offer a cast-iron guarantee against acquiring tenants with adverse qualities, but does improve the odds considerably.

Once a tenant has signed an agreement and is occupying the property, it may be very difficult and costly to deal with any problems they then create. It is always better to reduce the opportunity for difficulties at the outset rather than be forced into dealing with them later.

RECEIVING AND ASSESSING APPLICATIONS

Inspect each application form thoroughly, checking that all questions have been answered and all necessary data supplied. There are various early warning signs which may cause you to be suspicious even before you undertake referencing. These include:

- No bank account details. Either the applicant does not have a bank account (very unusual) or the account is frequently in arrears and they are fearful of you procuring a reference.
- Incomplete data supplied. Either the applicant simply could not be bothered to identify the data or realises providing it could lead to their application being refused.
- Two or more items of information conflict. For example, the date of birth does not reflect the age given or is inconsistent with the age of the person who attended the viewing.
- Failing to provide copies of requested identification documents.
- Applicants who are self-employed but fail to give verifiable evidence of occupation or financial status.
- Applicants who urge you to process their application quickly and offer to pay an early deposit and rent in advance prior to or whilst referencing.
- The application is unsigned or initialled only. The signature should be in the same form as seen on the identification documents.
- One or more application forms missing from the list of individuals wishing to become joint-tenants. Are the cohabiters a stable group?

If there is nothing suspicious about the form received, if you are content with details given and satisfied with the notes you made on the day of viewing, move on to the next question regarding the applicant:

Can they afford the rent?

It is extremely unlikely that you will gain access to the multitude of variables affecting the applicant's financial circumstances at this early stage. Nonetheless, there is a simple but effective calculation to assess suitability. It is one that many reference companies, mortgage lenders and credit agencies adopt as a rough guide:

Monthly rent x 30 = Minimum annual salary

For example, a monthly rent of £550 multiplied by 30 equals £16,500. If the applicant's annual salary is £18,000 then they should be able to afford the rent. However, if their salary is only £15,000 he may find it a strain to meet the rent each month. Although this calculation does not consider specific outgoings or the personal circumstances of each applicant, it is useful as a general guide and I have personally found it to be very effective.

DISCRIMINATION

You must not discriminate on the grounds of:

◆ race and ethnic background
◆ sex
◆ religion
◆ disability.

The Human Rights Act and other anti-discrimination laws prevent landlords from disqualifying tenants under any of the above grounds and severe penalties can be imposed on any that do. You are advised to maintain adequate records showing how decisions about tenancy applications are made and, specifically, why particular applicants are refused.

EMPLOYING A REFERENCE AGENCY

Employing a reference agency is the easiest and often the quickest way to obtain results, but of course there is a cost involved; most charge around £30 for a standard service.

A word of caution: if you intend employing an agency, check the nature of details they will require from applicants. Many have their own style of application form and will insist on this being used for all submissions. Acquire copies in advance to give to your prospective tenants. An example of the information required by professional reference agencies is given in the sample form, which can be found as an Appendix at the back of this book (my thanks to Marie Scott and all at **www.forlandlords.co.uk** for supplying this useful document).

Most referencing companies target their services to letting agents rather than to individual private sector landlords. The following are a few who currently offer professional assistance to both:

Experian Tenant Verifier
Verifer Services – West One, Riverleen House, Electric Avenue, Nottingham NG8 1RH.
Tel: 0115 901 6004
E-mail: verifier.services@uk.experian.com
Website: **www.tenantverifier.com**

ForLandlords
Becor House, Green Lane, Lincoln LN6 7DL.
Tel: 0870 703 9009
E-mail: info@forlandlords.co.uk
Website: **www.forlandlords.co.uk**

LandlordZone
Parkmatic Publications Ltd, 2 Moor Way, Hawkshaw, Lancashire BL8 4LF.
Tel: 0870 765 4420
E-mail: editor@landlordzone.co.uk
Website: **www.landlordzone.co.uk/verify.htm**

Leaseguard Ltd
Claremont Lodge, 24 Auchingramont Road, Hamilton ML3 6JT.
Tel: 0845 345 1705
E-mail: referencing@leaseguard.co.uk
Website: **www.leaseguard.co.uk**

LETsure Tenant Assessment
Lumley Letsure Limited, Granite House, 31 Stockwell Street, Glasgow G1 4RZ.
Tel: 08700 777808
E-mail: info@letsure.co.uk
Website: **www.letsure.co.uk**

Paragon Advance
4–5 The Briars, Waterberry Drive, Waterlooville, Hants PO7 7YH.
Tel: 08700 732235
E-mail: referencing@paragonadvance.com
Website: **www.paragonadvance.com**

LetSafe now offer a tenant screening service for landlords wishing to undertake checks on applicants from overseas. Traditionally, many potentially good tenants have been refused accommodation because credit searches and references could not be taken up quickly or safely. LetSafe claim they can now undertake a search of every business and individual globally on a unique database, which is updated daily. The new service is offered in conjunction with LetSafe's Rent Guarantee insurance policies. For more information telephone 0870 770 4602 or visit **www.letsafe.net**

The 'do-it-yourself' approach to tenant-referencing involves little more than a few letters and telephone calls and, although it may take a little longer, it will save the cost of a professional service.

OBTAINING AN EMPLOYMENT REFERENCE

Checking an applicant's employment status is essential as some may give false or misleading information, particularly with regard to their length and security of contract and their salary. Figure 6 is an example of the letter you should send to the employer. Attach a copy of the completed application form as it contains an authority for the employer to reply and include a stamped addressed envelope to encourage a faster response.

OBTAINING A BANK REFERENCE

These are the most awkward and frustrating of references you will need to obtain. Awkward because the details supplied by the applicant must be accurate and exact otherwise the bank will not respond with any useful information. Frustrating because, even if the data is correct, the bank is likely to take an inordinate amount of time to reply and they rarely give a straightforward answer. They are reluctant to appear disparaging about customers and therefore write in a vague and non-committal manner. This requires a landlord to read between the lines.

A bank might respond by stating they '*are surprised the customer has considered agreeing to a regular expense of this size*'. This implies that the applicant has enough going out of his account already and any additions would strain their resources. Always read a bank reference reply several times and make sure you fully appreciate what is being said.

Be aware that most banks charge a fee for references. Consider obtaining, in advance, a mandate from the applicant allowing the fee to be deducted from their account. This speeds up the process and shows that the applicant has the commitment and confidence to proceed. Figure 7 is an example of a mandate which should be supplied to interested viewers together with the application form. Make sure that this is returned to you duly completed and signed so that a bank reference can be obtained.

Figure 8 is an example of the letter to the bank. Attach the applicant's mandate to the letter. There is no need to provide a reply envelope with this request.

OBTAINING CREDIT REFERENCES

A credit reference is a report compiled by an agency with access to public record data and other private information. This includes details about:

◆ county court judgements (CCJs)
◆ credit and hire-purchase history
◆ electoral roll data
◆ information on bankruptcy and loan repayments.

(Your name, address and telephone/fax numbers)

(Name and address of employer)

(Date)

Dear

Ref: (Name of applicant)

The person named above has applied for a residential tenancy from me at £(rent) per month and has given me the authority to contact you for a reference. Please would you respond by answering the following questions and return as soon as possible using the SAE provided.

1. What is his/her annual salary?   £_____

2. Is he/she on a permanent contract with you?   YES ☐ NO ☐

3. How long has he/she been employed by you?   _____

4. Do you consider him/her to be a reliable,
   honest and trustworthy employee?   YES ☐ NO ☐

5. Do you consider his/her salary is sufficient to
   pay the monthly rent of £(rent) given other
   deductions and outgoings?   YES ☐ NO ☐

All information given will be treated in the strictest confidence. Thank you for your time and co-operation in regard to this matter.

PLEASE SIGN HERE

YOUR TITLE/POST HELD   _____

Yours sincerely

Fig. 6. Example of an employment reference request.

The various facts and figures are collated to provide lenders, banks and others with an assessment of an individual's financial history to date. A credit reference enables you to make an objective decision about the level of risk involved in offering a rental agreement to the applicant. Credit references can be obtained from most of the aforementioned companies and charges vary according to the type of report required.

OBTAINING A LANDLORD'S REFERENCE

If the applicant is currently living in rented accommodation, it is important to obtain a reference from his landlord. Use Figure 6 as a template, but substitute the following questions:

- How long is/was the applicant a tenant of yours?
- What is/was the monthly rent being paid?
- Was this rent paid in full and on time each month?
- Were there any periods where the rent was in arrears?
- Is the rent currently in arrears?
- Has the applicant cared properly for the property and its contents?
- Would you accept the applicant as a tenant again?

Some applicants may give false information, possibly because there has been a poor tenant/landlord relationship. The applicant might, for example, give a friend's details instead of their landlord's. One way of checking this is to telephone the landlord acting in the manner of someone searching for rented property. If the response is awkward or confused, you can be fairly certain you are not talking to the applicant's landlord. Seeking a reference would therefore be pointless.

VERIFYING THE HOME ADDRESS

It is important to check that the applicant's given address details are their permanent and registered place of residence. If not, then there will be no record of them having paid utility bills (and therefore no history of good or bad payment) and it will be difficult to trace CCJs without an address by which they can be identified. A reference company will check these facts for you.

It is possible to undertake this investigation using the internet, though most sites charge for their services. **www.192.com** offer an alternative where you can participate in surveys and questionnaires, thereby gaining enough credits to complete an electoral roll search. They also offer an electoral roll search at a nominal charge.

BANK MANDATE

NAME   _____ (Applicant)

ADDRESS _____ (Applicant's home address)

           _____

TO: The Manager

        _____ (Bank name)

        _____ (Address of bank)

        _____

        _____

(Date)

Dear Sir/Madam,

I/we hereby authorise you to provide information to (landlord's name) of (landlord's postal address) as requested by their letter attached. I/we understand there will be a charge for this and I/we authorise you to deduct the appropriate sum from my/our account held with you, the details of which are:

NAME OF ACCOUNT_____

ACCOUNT NUMBER_____

Please send your reply direct to (landlord's name) at their address as soon as possible.

Yours faithfully,

_____
Account holder's signature(s)

Fig. 7. Example of an applicant's bank mandate.

(Your name, address and telephone/fax numbers)

(Name and address of bank)

(Date)

Dear

Ref: (Name of Applicant)

The person named above has applied for a residential tenancy from me at £(rent) per month and has given me the authority to contact you for a reference. Please would you respond by answering the following questions. The applicant has given authority for any charge relating to this reference to be deducted from his account held with you (please see the attached mandate).

1. The applicant intends to pay a deposit of £(deposit) plus rent of £(rent) per month. Do you consider he/she is able to meet these commitments?

    _____

2. Are you aware of any current, impending or future payments that may cause him/her to have difficulty in meeting the regular monthly rent payment?

    _____

3. Are there any additional comments you wish to make relating to the applicant's financial history or circumstances, with regard to his/her application for a tenancy at the rent stated? If so, please write them here.

    _____

All information given will be treated in the strictest confidence. Thank you for your time and co-operation in regard to this matter.

Yours sincerely

Fig. 8. Example of a bank reference request.

It is also worth asking the applicant to provide the originals (not copies) of two recently paid utility bills (gas, electric, water and/or council tax) displaying their name and address. Check the details against the application form to ensure accuracy.

CHARGING COSTS TO THE APPLICANT

It is perfectly legal for a landlord to charge administrative costs to an applicant. The elements making up this fee might include:

- postage
- telephone calls
- professional referencing services and credit check
- time given to dealing with the application
- photocopying and/or printing of documents.

The applicant *must* be made fully aware of this charge *before* applying for a tenancy. It must also be made quite clear that the fee is non-refundable, regardless of the outcome of the application. A suitable explanation could be included on the application form together with a request for payment in full. Although many landlords charge an administration fee, it can discourage applicants. Before imposing the levy, consider the level of (tenant) supply and (property) demand at the time.

GUARANTORS

There are various reasons why referencing can fail to provide adequate results. The applicant may not have registered with utility companies, having only recently settled in the country. They may be temporarily working in the UK, but their family and permanent home could be overseas. Or this may be their first application for accommodation away from the parental home. In all of these situations, the would-be tenant's financial history and suitability may be difficult to verify and acquiring a guarantor will therefore be essential.

A **surety guarantor** guarantees the payment of rent and/or other obligations agreed between tenant and landlord. The guarantor becomes legally liable for these contractual commitments if the tenant defaults on payment, causes damage, or breaks some other pertinent condition of tenancy. The guarantor should be referenced in the same manner and to the same degree as an actual tenant. A guarantor agreement is then completed and signed, preferably at the same time as the tenancy agreement. This should always be undertaken face-to-face and with proof of identity to ensure the referenced guarantor is the same person signing the document.

Guarantor agreements can be obtained from most law stationers or alternatively one can be devised for you by a solicitor. Most forms prescribe liability during the initial, fixed term of the tenancy (the contractual period) but *not* for any continuation of the term or renewal of tenancy. It is therefore important to consult with your legal adviser, before completing the form, to ensure suitable clauses are inserted or amendments made that provide for all eventualities arising at the end of the term.

Many landlords and letting-agents accept guarantors routinely because of the nature of their business and rarely report problems in doing so. However, guarantors can frustrate what is already a very complex procedure and, at best, they will create additional administration and a protracted commencement to the tenancy. Novice landlords are best advised to seek an alternative tenant whose reference results are satisfactory, eliminating any need for a guarantor.

COMPANY-LET REFERENCING

If the tenant is to be a company, it is important to undertake full referencing to verify its financial condition and legal status. Professional referencing will ordinarily examine the company's creditworthiness, registered address, limited company status, accounting history and turnover. The agencies listed previously all provide this service.

SUMMARY

♦ Thoroughly inspect all returned application forms. Check that all sections have been completed and all questions fully answered. Be suspicious of any missing information.
♦ Before starting the reference process, assess whether the applicant can afford the rent being asked and determine whether they satisfy your tenant criteria.
♦ Conduct *full* referencing. Consider the advantages of employing an agency to undertake it.
♦ Decide in advance whether to charge administrative costs.
♦ Always reference a guarantor to the same degree as the original applicant.

CHAPTER EIGHT

The Law of Tenancy

In this chapter:

- ◆ the Housing Acts
- ◆ confirming permission to let
- ◆ tenancy or licence?
- ◆ assured and assured shorthold tenancies
- ◆ unfair tenancy terms
- ◆ obtaining sample tenancy agreements
- ◆ joint tenancies
- ◆ company-let agreements.

The law affecting landlords in England and Wales is vast and complex. A book of this size cannot explain all the regulations involved nor should it be considered a definitive guide to the various individual situations that may be encountered. Both novice and experienced landlords are advised to consult a solicitor specialised in housing law who can counsel on specific problems. Although limited by necessity, this chapter provides a general guide to the legislation and is intended to help instil a greater understanding of what is involved.

THE HOUSING ACTS

These provide the legal framework through which private residential tenancies are created and managed, and contain the definitions, rules and procedures affecting landlords and tenants in England and Wales. The Housing Acts offer statutory protection to both parties and deal with matters including harassment, eviction, tenancy termination, possession rights, tenant deposit protection, rent increases and arrears.

The Housing Act 1988 introduced two types of tenancy – '**assured**' and '**assured shorthold**' – the latter being the most commonly used. Important changes made by the Housing Act 1996 mean that all tenancies created after 28 February 1997 are automatically the assured shorthold type, unless they fail to meet the criteria or the tenant was issued with an appropriate notice stating otherwise (see below). As this book is concerned only with new tenancies, it describes the procedures and regulations dictated by the Acts above only. For older-style tenancies, started prior to 28 February 1997, landlords are advised to seek professional advice. The Housing Acts are only part of the law involved. There is other legislation, such as that affecting furnishings described in Chapter 3, which combine to make up the whole picture.

CONFIRMING PERMISSION TO LET

Before completing the tenancy agreement, you must confirm you have all the necessary documents that legally authorise you to proceed. Where the property to be let has been bought with a **mortgage** you should:

◆ inform the lender *in advance* and *obtain written permission* to create a tenancy in accordance with any contractual obligation to do so; and

◆ incorporate any mandatory demands or restrictions of use, made by the lender, into the tenancy agreement; and

◆ inform the proposed tenant that the property is mortgaged and explain the implications for them (reference can be made in the tenancy agreement to an appropriate note for the purpose of clarity).

Should you fail to meet mortgage payments, the lender may seek to repossess the property. The tenant is unlikely to have any legal right to continue occupying it, but could take proceedings against you for being evicted. This may differ where the lender has recognised the existence of the tenancy and has agreed to it or where the tenancy was entered into before the mortgage began. Most lenders insist on prior notice being issued to tenants (under Grounds 1 and 2 of Schedule 2 of the Housing Act 1988). It is common practice for such notice to be included within the body of the tenancy agreement.

Where the property to be let is **leasehold**, you should also apply for permission from the headlessor. Always obtain such authority in writing *before* completing the tenancy agreement.

It is important to check with your local authority whether an accreditation or licensing scheme operates in the area you intend letting your property (see information on 'selective licensing' in Chapter 1). Proceeding to let without having a licence (where one is required) is extremely perilous and can result in a fine being imposed of up to £20,000.

TENANCY OR LICENCE?

Certain conditions must be met in order that a tenancy can be created. The main criterion is that the tenant has *exclusive* use of the accommodation. For example, if you are intending to let a room in your own home or require unrestricted access to the room then it is likely to be a **licence to occupy**, rather than a tenancy.

Resident landlords cannot usually create an assured or an assured shorthold tenancy and so different rules and rights will apply to both the landlord and occupier. It is not necessary for you to share part of the dwelling with the occupier to be classed as a resident landlord. In some circumstances, merely living in the same building will be enough!

For more information, obtain the free booklet *Letting Rooms in Your Own Home – A Guide for Landlords and Tenants* available from Communities and Local Government. A pdf download of the booklet can be obtained from **www.communities.gov.uk/embedded_object.asp?id = 1508399** or a paper version is available by writing to Communities and Local Government Publications, PO Box 236, Wetherby, West Yorkshire LS23 7NB or by telephoning 0870 122 6236.

ASSURED AND ASSURED SHORTHOLD TENANCIES

This book intends that you create the assured shorthold type of tenancy because it provides the landlord and tenant with mutual benefits. The landlord has a greater degree of security and an easier means of regaining possession at the end of the fixed term. The tenant has a guaranteed period of occupation, providing they maintain rent payments and other tenancy commitments. The descriptions here refer only to tenancies starting after 28 February 1997.

Changes made by the Housing Act 1996 made the creation of an assured shorthold tenancy (AST) very simple and straightforward. In effect, it reversed the prior situation whereby notice had to be served in a prescribed form to create one. It is prudent for us to examine more closely what criteria must exist for an AST to be created and, importantly, what the difference is between the two types.

'Assured' type

This is sometimes referred to as an 'ordinary' or 'full' assured tenancy. The tenant must receive a notice from the landlord stating that it is to be an assured tenancy *before* it begins. If no notice is issued, then it cannot be of this type. Ordinary assured tenants enjoy greater security of tenure. They can occupy the property for an undetermined period and the landlord can only regain possession if they satisfy the courts that certain 'grounds' exist. They have no automatic right to repossess the property just because the tenancy has come to an end. Tenants also have the right to apply for a rent assessment to be conducted and, once assessed, the landlord cannot charge more than the maximum determined.

'Assured shorthold' type

These exist for a fixed period. The tenant does not enjoy indefinite security of tenure. Tenants can apply for a rent assessment during the initial fixed term. Landlords can regain possession of their property at the end of the fixed term or, if the term is less than six months, after six months from the start of tenancy providing appropriate notice is issued to the tenant. If that seems very complicated, don't worry, it will be explained in more detail later. For now it is enough to understand that an AST gives the landlord greater legal powers to obtain possession of the property at the end of the tenancy term. **The tenancy cannot be an assured shorthold if**:

♦ It is a business letting.
♦ It is a holiday let.
♦ It is not the tenant's only or main residence.
♦ The landlord is classed as a resident landlord.
♦ The tenancy began before 15 January 1989.
♦ The tenant is not an individual (this does not exclude joint-tenants).
♦ There is no rent charged or the rent is less than two thirds of the rateable value of the property or is £250 or less a year (£1,000 or less in Greater London).
♦ The rent charged exceeds £25,000 per year.
♦ It includes agricultural land of two acres or more or is an agricultural holding.
♦ The premises are licensed to sell or consume alcohol.
♦ It is not being let as a separate dwelling.
♦ The landlord is an educational body, the Crown or a government department, a local authority, housing action trust, or one of several other statutory bodies or a mutual housing association.
♦ It fails to meet the criteria and definitions laid down in the Housing Act 1988 (as amended by the Housing Act 1996).

UNFAIR TENANCY TERMS

It is no longer safe to write into a tenancy agreement anything that contravenes the OFT's guidelines on unfair tenancy terms. This means that all tenancy agreements must be worded carefully and with due regard to pertinent legislation. To comply, tenancy agreements:

♦ Must be written without ambiguity and in plain language that tenants are able to understand.
♦ Must not force unreasonable prohibitions on tenants. For example, a clause that states '*the tenant must not keep inflammable materials on the premises*' prohibits them from storing a box of matches. This is clearly not reasonable and should be better phrased to guard against the storage of materials presenting a genuine fire hazard.

◆ Must not force unreasonable obligations on tenants. For example, a clause which states *'the tenant must keep the furnishings clean and dusted at all times'* is unreasonable, as very few people keep their home dust-free at all times.

◆ Should not assume a tenant's comprehension of what is written. For example, the declaration *'I have read and fully understand...'* is unsafe because in practice few tenants read or fully understand all aspects of a tenancy agreement. Declarations might be more acceptable if they begin with *'The tenant **should** read and understand the terms before signing...'*.

◆ Must not exclude the tenant from assigning or subletting. Landlords have a vested interest in preventing their property falling into the hands of unsuitable sub-tenants but, without vetting them, how can they know whether they are unsuitable or not? Global terms are likely to be unacceptable in law, whereas a clause that allows the tenant to sublet in certain circumstances and following a set procedure is more likely to gain favour.

These are just a few of the conditions and examples given in the OFT guide. There are additional **contract** and **consumer** laws that affect the way in which tenancy agreements are worded and the clauses they can legally contain. It is also worth bearing in mind that, whatever is written into an agreement, statute law takes precedence. A tenancy agreement clause cannot override the legal protection afforded to tenants. However, it may frustrate, confuse or invalidate the entire agreement if it has to be submitted to the courts as evidence. Agreements should always be approved by a solicitor experienced in this area of law before being used, regardless of the source.

OBTAINING SAMPLE TENANCY AGREEMENTS

There is a wide range of pre-printed AST agreements available at varying prices. It is important to confirm that any purchased suit the circumstances for which they are intended and that they are up-to-date with current legislation. All of the following supply standard forms that can be purchased by telephone:

CompactLaw
Tel: 0845 166 8711

Stat Plus Group
Tel: 0845 606 1100

Oyez Legal Forms
Tel: 0870 737 7370

The Letting Centre
Tel: 01223 568568

ASTs can also be obtained over the internet as downloads or as interactive printable forms or mail order at the following sites (prices accurate at time of inspection):

www.buytolet4sale.com (£9.99)
www.clickdocs.co.uk (£26.32)

www.compactlaw.co.uk (£15.00)
www.freelawyer.co.uk (£30.00)
www.landlordzone.co.uk (£30.00)
www.lawpack.co.uk (£14.99)
www.legalhelpers.co.uk (£30.00)
www.legalshop.co.uk (£30.00)
www.lettings-landlords.co.uk (£4.50)
www.oyezformslink.co.uk (£5.00)
www.rla.org.uk (£5.00)
www.tenant-agreement.co.uk (£9.97)

Note: Some of the above include various additional forms, guidance notes, other documents or services within the price.

JOINT TENANCIES

A joint tenancy is one in which the occupants of the same dwelling consist of two or more tenants that are named on the same tenancy agreement. In addition to the warning given about creating a House in Multiple Occupation (see Chapter 1), there are additional problems associated with joint tenancies. These include:

◆ A situation where one of the tenants decides to leave during the term of the tenancy, leaving those remaining to pay the rent or to agree a replacement with the landlord. The former may cause hardship to the tenant(s), resulting in rent arrears; to be legally safe, the latter involves ending the first tenancy and starting a new one, with resulting additional administration and referencing costs. Difficulties can also arise over deposit refunds and who should receive what and when. In addition, during a periodic tenancy, if one tenant issues Notice to Quit then it becomes binding on all other joint tenants, even if they do not agree.

◆ Although joint tenants are usually deemed to be **severally liable** for the rent (i.e., each is equally responsible for the entire sum), in practice tenants share a property because they need to combine incomes to afford the rent. So, if one tenant loses their job or experiences a strain on their resources, the rent may not be paid in full unless the others can (and want) to make up the difference.

◆ Joint tenants who are friends or colleagues, rather than partners, may be cohabiting for the first time and living together may cause unexpected friction. This is particularly likely when the joint tenants are young and have recently moved out of the parental home. The letting may have been requested for a fixed term of six months, but it may fall apart after just one!

When granting a joint tenancy, consider carefully the relationship between the parties and their ability to pay rent independently if things go wrong.

COMPANY-LET AGREEMENTS

Lettings to companies are outside the scope of the Housing Act 1988 and cannot be of the assured or assured shorthold type. This can be advantageous to landlords because these tenants do not enjoy the full statutory protection afforded to individuals. It is, however, important to identify how the accommodation will be used by the company to prevent potential problems arising.

Many do so to accommodate their employees in preference to using a hotel. The employees usually occupy the dwelling as licensees. In these circumstances, when the period of tenancy ends, the occupiers must vacate. However, if the company is allowed to conduct business from the premises, they can apply for protection using the Landlord and Tenant Act 1954; it is therefore important to guard against such activity. The landlord can also prevent the 1954 Act applying by keeping the tenancy term under six months (but not if a series of consecutive tenancies amount to 12 months or more).

Company-let agreements are more difficult to obtain, but some of the previously mentioned suppliers of ASTs also produce sample documents of this type.

SUMMARY

- ◆ Confirm that you have all the necessary written permissions to let from lenders and headlessors.
- ◆ Aim to provide an assured shorthold tenancy as this affords you greater legal protection, but ensure that you and your property meet the criteria contained in the Housing Act first.
- ◆ Obtain a sample agreement and ask your solicitor to ensure it complies with current legislation.
- ◆ Be aware of the potential difficulties of a joint tenancy.
- ◆ If you intend to provide a company letting, be certain the tenant does not use your property to conduct business and keep the term to a maximum of six months.

CHAPTER NINE

Starting the Tenancy

In this chapter:

- ◆ reserving the property
- ◆ deposit and rent payments
- ◆ informing utility companies
- ◆ postal security
- ◆ completing the tenancy agreement
- ◆ stamp duty
- ◆ check-in
- ◆ record-keeping.

Most people assume a tenancy starts on the day an agreement is signed; this is not necessarily true. Neither is it always the case when a tenant takes up occupation or starts paying rent. However, as the day of commencement determines other notable legal dates during and at the end of tenancy, misinterpreting it can lead to security of tenancy being afforded unintentionally to the tenant. This chapter deals with these issues and explains how to prevent problems arising.

RESERVING THE PROPERTY

Tenants occasionally ask landlords to reserve a property. It may be that references have yet to be taken up or they have other commitments causing a delay to immediate occupation, so they may offer to pay a holding fee or both rent and deposit in advance. Landlords need to be extremely cautious in this situation. The lure of money up-front is enticing, but accepting it can create a legally binding arrangement later regretted. The answer is to enter into a pre-tenancy agreement, drafted by your solicitor, which states clearly:

- ◆ the amount being paid;
- ◆ any non-refundable element or agreed deductions for administration, referencing, keeping the property empty, and other preparatory arrangements;
- ◆ the rights of each party to withdraw from proceeding;
- ◆ how the sum paid is to be defined if a tenancy is later granted, for example as full or part surety deposit; and

◆ that the payment is *not* an instalment of rent (because a court might otherwise decide that, even without a written agreement, a tenancy has already begun).

DEPOSIT AND RENT PAYMENTS

Taking a deposit

By concluding all the aspects of tenancy commencement *on the same day* and immediately prior to occupation, there will be less confusion and greater certainty regarding ongoing dates. This involves taking the deposit and first rent-period sums *and* signing the agreement *before* releasing keys. When preparing to accept a deposit, think about:

◆ **The amount**. Any amount of deposit can be demanded when granting an assured shorthold tenancy. Although one month's rent equivalent is usual, it may be inadequate as some tenants default on paying the last month's rent (leaving the landlord with no security to reimburse the cost of any damage). However, be cautious of accepting more than two months' rent equivalent as it may be construed as a **premium**, giving the tenant an automatic right to **assign** (transfer the tenancy to another person), unless it is specifically precluded by the agreement.

◆ **How it will be paid**. Cheques are not a secure form of payment. Insist on cash or a bank-draft.

The Tenancy Deposit Protection Rules (2007)

Tenancy deposit protection was introduced through the Housing Act 2004 and affects all assured shorthold tenancies that began on or after 6 April 2007. The legislation does not affect assured tenancies or other lettings outside the scope of the Housing Acts, such as a company let. The tenancy deposit protection rules effectively removed the prior control over surety sums being held and deductions being made direct by landlords and/or their agents.

Although landlords and/or their agents can still receive dilapidation deposit sums from tenants, such sums must be 'safeguarded' in one of a choice of approved schemes – the choice being dependent on whether a landlord is managing his own letting or undertaking it through a letting agent. The rules dictate the time limit by which landlords and agents must have handed over deposits to the appropriate scheme administrator from the start of tenancy, and inflict a strict regime on how any disputes will be handled at the end of tenancy, if there are damages to the property or its contents and the landlord wishes to claim such costs from the tenant(s).

During 2006, government awarded contracts to three companies to run tenancy deposit schemes from their introduction in April 2007. Currently, these are the only approved providers of tenancy deposit schemes in England and Wales.

Each scheme operates according to its target audience, who are either letting agents or individual landlords. Landlords only have one option, if they decide not to follow the tenancy deposit scheme rules – they can choose to pursue one of the alternative insurance policy opt-out schemes now entering the market or decide not to collect any kind of surety deposit from their tenants. However, if they use a letting agent, landlords will have no choice as their agent will have had to register themselves with an appropriate scheme, which in turn will dictate what their clients can and cannot do regarding deposits.

The choice over which of the tenancy deposit schemes to adopt will impact on your tenancy agreement. It is vital the agreement is worded to accommodate the rules and requirements of the appropriate scheme (each scheme imposes mandatory tenancy agreement clauses).

The government-approved schemes are as follows.

The custodial scheme

Computershare Investor Services plc run the only custodial deposit scheme, which is available to both landlords and letting agents. The landlord or agent collects a deposit from a tenant and then hands it over to the scheme administrators. The landlord or agent must provide the tenant with details of the scheme being used within 14 days of receiving the deposit funds. There are no costs associated with this particular scheme, as interest accrued on deposit sums is used to finance its running costs, with any surplus paid to either the tenant or landlord at the end of the term, depending on provisions contained in the tenancy agreement.

When the tenancy reaches expiry, the tenant and landlord can agree how to divide deposit amounts between them – assuming there is evidence of damage to the property or other associated tenant-liable expenses incurred by the landlord. Where an agreement is reached, the deposit sums must be returned within ten days. However, if the tenant and landlord cannot agree, the scheme will hold on to the deposit until such time as the dispute resolution service or courts decide what should be done. The Chartered Institute of Arbitrators have been approved to provide a mandatory Alternative Dispute Resolution Service under such circumstances.

The two insurance-based deposit schemes

These schemes are operated by two different companies and, despite having principally the same mechanism, one is intended mainly for access by landlords whilst the other is mainly for letting agents. The Dispute Service Limited runs the insurance-based scheme and the associated arbitration service for letting agents. Tenancy Deposit Solutions Limited runs a very similar scheme for individual landlords, which is sponsored by the National Landlords' Association (administered by Hamilton Fraser Insurance). The Chartered Institute of Arbitrators operate the approved alternative dispute resolution service for the landlords' scheme.

Under both schemes, the tenant pays his or her deposit to the landlord or letting agent, who then retains it together with any interest it attracts in accordance with the tenancy agreement provisions. The landlord or agent then pays an insurance premium in accordance with the relevant scheme provider's instructions. The insurance policy protects the tenant's deposit against failure by the landlord or agent to return it by the due date at the end of tenancy. There are costs associated with both insurance-based schemes and these are borne by the landlord or letting agent. Tenants must be given details of the relevant scheme within 14 days of handing over their deposit.

At tenancy expiry, the landlord or agent and tenant must agree how the deposit is to be divided, if at all. The deposit – or part thereof – is then refunded to the tenant. If any amount is disputed, the landlord or agent must pay the disputed amount to the scheme provider, who will keep it until the dispute is resolved.

Penalties for failing to observe tenancy deposit protection law

The law of tenancy deposit protection is absolute and landlords are strongly advised to follow the rules 'to the letter' to avoid severe repercussions. Tenants are being advised, and in some cases assisted and encouraged, to pursue civil action against landlords who do not keep to the rules. Where courts find there is a case to answer, they can award up to three times the amount of the deposit as a fine against the landlord, which the tenant then receives in compensation *and* prohibit the landlord from issuing a valid Section 21 notice. The tenancy cannot be brought to an end without a valid Section 21 notice, which means under such circumstances the tenant can remain in occupation for as long as he or she wishes.

Further information

Details of and contact information for the various approved tenancy deposit protection companies, scheme operators and arbitration services can be found under the Useful Information section at the back of this book. Additional and more detailed information on the tenancy deposit protection rules, how to access the schemes and how they operate can be viewed at the following internet addresses:

- **www.depositprotection.com** (for the custodial scheme)
- **www.tds.gb.com** (for the insurance-based scheme intended mainly for letting agents)
- **www.mydeposits.co.uk** (for the insurance-based scheme intended mainly for landlords).

Setting up rent payments

Rent is paid in advance, therefore a sum covering the first period should be collected in cash or by bank-draft before signing the tenancy agreement. Ongoing rent payments can be arranged by completing a standing-order mandate.

INFORMING UTILITY COMPANIES

Utility companies will only send bills to the tenant *in his or her name* if they are informed about the change of liability. It is therefore important to take meter readings and contact them as soon as tenancy starts (see Figures 9 to 13 for sample letters). The preferred method is to telephone all companies on the commencement date and then confirm immediately in writing, taking copies for the tenant and your files. Where appropriate, contact each of the following:

- local authority council-tax office
- gas supplier
- electricity supplier
- water supplier
- telecommunication company – if the telephone line is in your name, have it disconnected in advance of the tenancy start date to confirm service termination.

POSTAL SECURITY

In time, you may come to trust your tenants. For now, you must consider them as strangers with the skill and desire to commit criminal acts against you. To prevent potential fraud and/or theft, ensure no mail is delivered to the property containing details of your bank accounts, credit cards, driving licence, or other financial and identification data.

STANDING ORDER MANDATE

TO:- (Tenant's Bank Address)

_____ Bank

_____

_____

Post Code _____

PLEASE PAY:- (Landlord Details)

Bank Name	Branch
Account Number	Sort Code
Beneficiary (Account Name)	

THE SUM OF:- (Rent Details)

Amount Of Rent £	Written In Words

COMMENCING:- First Payment Date

AND ON THE _____ OF EVERY _____ THEREAFTER UNTIL YOU RECEIVE FURTHER NOTICE FROM ME IN WRITING

DEBITING MY ACCOUNT:- (Tenant's Account Details)

Account Name	Account Number

SIGNATURE:- _____ **DATE:** _____

NAME IN CAPITALS:- _____

Fig. 9. Sample bank mandate for rent payments.

(Your name, address and telephone/fax numbers)

(Name and address of Council Tax office)

(Date)

Dear

Ref: (Let property address and post code)

Property Reference Number:
(Shown on the last statement received)

I write to inform you that the above property has been let to new tenants from today. The tenant(s) is/are responsible for paying council tax relating to the property. The tenant(s) details are:

Tenant(s) Name(s):

**Council Tax Liability
Commenced On:**

**Tenant(s) Prior
Address:**

Please amend your records accordingly.

Yours sincerely,

Fig. 10. Sample letter for council tax liability.

(Your name, address and telephone/fax numbers)

(Name and address of company supplying gas)

(Date)

Dear

Ref: (Let property address and post code)

Customer Reference Number:
(Shown on the last statement received)

I write to inform you that the above property has been let to new tenants from today. The tenant(s) is/are responsible for paying all charges relating to the supply and consumption of gas at the property. The tenant(s) details are:

Tenant(s) Name(s):

**Gas Charges Liability
Commenced On:**

**Tenant(s) Prior
Address:**

Meter reading taken today:

Please amend your records accordingly.

Yours sincerely,

Fig. 11. Sample letter for gas supply liability.

(Your name, address and telephone/fax numbers)

(Name and address of company supplying electricity)

(Date)

Dear

Ref: (Let property address and post code) _____

Customer Reference Number:
(Shown on the last statement received)

I write to inform you that the above property has been let to new tenants from today. The tenant(s) is/are responsible for paying all charges relating to the supply and consumption of electricity at the property. The tenant(s) details are:

Tenant(s) Name(s):

**Electricity Charges
Liability Commenced On:**

**Tenant(s) Prior
Address:**

Meter reading(s) taken today:

NORMAL   OFF-PEAK

Please amend your records accordingly.

Yours sincerely,

Fig. 12. Sample letter for electricity supply liability.

(Your name, address and telephone/fax numbers)

(Name and address of the water authority)

(Date)

Dear

Ref: (Let property address and post code)

Reference Number:
(Shown on the last statement received)

I write to inform you that new occupiers have moved into the property above and are responsible for all water and sewerage charges from today. The details are:

Tenant(s) Name(s):

**Water Charges
Liability Commenced On:**

**Tenant(s) Prior
Address:**

Meter Reading Taken Today:
(if property is metered)

Please amend your records accordingly.

Yours sincerely,

Fig. 13. Sample letter for water supply liability.

COMPLETING THE TENANCY AGREEMENT

Whilst AST agreements can vary in the number, wording and diversity of terms and conditions forming the bulk of the document, most require similar information to be entered on the first page. This will usually include:

- **Property address**: means the let property. Write the full address and post code.
- **Landlord**: means you. Write your name in full (and any co-owner).
- **Landlord's address**: means the address in England or Wales for tenants to contact you in writing, report damage or for an emergency.
- **Tenant**: means those who applied to rent the property from you. This may be an individual, a couple or a group. In each case, write their full name(s). Remember that a company letting cannot be an assured shorthold tenancy. Where a company let agreement is being used, be certain to enter the full *registered* name of the company.
- **Tenant's address**: means the registered prior address(es). In the case of a company letting, the address should be the *registered* head office address or (for limited companies) the address registered at Company House.
- **Term**: means the fixed period of tenancy being granted. For reasons we will discuss later, it is advised you provide a minimum of six months (enter in words).
- **Beginning on**: means the first day of tenancy and from when rent becomes due (not necessarily the occupation date). To prevent confusion and possible complications arising later in the tenancy, avoid the 1st, 28th, 29th, 30th and 31st as commencement dates as these can be problematic when calculating the end-of-tenancy and rent-due dates. For example, a six-month tenancy starting on 30 August will expire on 28 February, except during a leap-year when it will be the 29 February.
- **Rent**: means the sum covering the period (usually a weekly, monthly or quarterly amount).
- **Payable on**: means the date in the month or day of the week that rent becomes due. If a tenancy starts on 6 July then subsequent monthly rent payments fall due on the 6th of each month. Some landlords opt to change the 'rent collection date' to the start or end of the month for convenience, but note that confusion can arise if arrears build up and formal notice needs to be given.
- **Deposit**: means the sum received as surety against dilapidations arising at the end of tenancy.
- **Date**: means the date the tenancy agreement is signed, which may be earlier but not any later than the day tenancy starts.

Two identical copies of the tenancy agreement will be required and the exact same data must be entered on each one. One copy is **the Agreement**, issued to the tenant(s); the other is **the Counterpart**, retained by the landlord. The significance of these will become clear later in this chapter.

Always use blue or black ink and write in block capitals for clarity. The agreement should confirm that it comprises the details above, the terms and conditions given and the inventory attached. Formal completion (signing) of the agreement *can* be undertaken in advance of the tenancy starting, but it is best done at the property on the day of tenancy commencement and with all parties present (see 'Check-in' below).

STAMP DUTY LAND TAX

All tenancies created after 1 December 2003 become liable for Stamp Duty Land Tax (SDLT) payable to HM Revenue & Customs. This replaces the previous Stamp Duty system whereby most tenancy documents had to be physically stamped by the tax office. The introduction of SDLT means that most residential tenancies do not incur tax and the system is therefore much easier to apply by landlords and their tenants.

SDLT only becomes due for tenancies with more than £125,000 accrued rent (known as the lease value) per tenancy period. This rate was accurate up to 1 August 2007. A tenancy period includes renewals and continuous periodic periods, so a 12-month tenancy renewed each year for five years and with a rent *exceeding* £2,083.33 per month, *would* become liable for SDLT (but see below).

Calculating the amount payable is somewhat more difficult than the prior system, because a reduction of the *lease value* is made to take account of *net present value* (NPV). Landlords who wish to learn more about SDLT and adjusting for NPV can visit **www.hmrc.gov.uk/so** where full details are listed. The site also has a useful SDLT calculator.

The good news is that the responsibility for paying SDLT falls on the tenant, so there are no dire consequences for failing to comprehend the system from the landlord's point of view. However, good practice dictates you should inform your tenant(s) of their liability, if appropriate, and advise where they can acquire further guidance. The Stamp Office Helpline is available (weekdays) on 0845 603 0135.

CHECK-IN

Once a date has been agreed for the tenancy to start, it should not be changed unless there are exceptional circumstances. The day before the appointment, telephone the tenant(s) and confirm they are aware:

- ◆ of the tenancy commencement date and appointment time;
- ◆ that they must have the deposit and rent in cash or bank-draft;
- ◆ that it will take approximately one hour to complete the check-in procedure;
- ◆ that all applicants must attend the appointment.

Start the tenancy following the procedure below in order:

1. Give both copies of the inventory and ask tenants to verify its accuracy by inspecting the property and its contents. Explain that any additional comments or observations can be entered on the documents in the spaces provided. The tenants should sign and date *both* copies of the inventory. The landlord signs only the **original**, which is then given to and retained by the tenants. The landlord keeps the copy that does *not* have his or her signature.

2. Collect the rent and deposit. No receipt is required as the amounts are confirmed as paid in the tenancy agreement. If the rent is to be paid weekly, you must provide a rent book (available from stationers). Obtain the tenants' signatures on the standing-order mandate for ongoing rent payments.

3. Give the tenants both copies of the AST agreement. Ask them to read through it and answer any queries. The tenants sign and date *one* copy (endorsed as the **counterpart**), retained by the landlord. The landlord signs *one* copy only (the **original** agreement), retained by the tenants. This completes the formal process.

4. It is useful to have a witness to the signing of legal documents to help confirm authenticity of the signatures if later disputed. This is not, however, a legal requirement.

5. Supply the tenants with copies of all appliance manuals, instructions and any other documents relating to the property.

6. Explain the operation of intruder alarms, security devices, hot water and heating systems.

7. Explain where emergency shut-off valves, stop-taps and meters are located for gas, electricity and water.

8. Provide copies of letters sent to utility companies.

9. Hand keys over.

10. Advise the tenants of your intention to conduct inspections every three months and that advance written notice will be given when each becomes due. Ensure this is provided for in the tenancy agreement.

11. Explain their legal responsibility to pay Stamp Duty Land Tax (if applicable) and inform them where they can get more information about it.

12. Provide the tenant(s) with a copy of the up-to-date gas safety certificate and obtain a receipt from the tenant(s) confirming they have been issued with it.

13. Within 14 days of receiving the deposit sum, provide the tenant(s) with written details of the deposit protection scheme being used and, if appropriate, pass the sum on to the scheme administrators or pay the insurance premium required in accordance with the relevant scheme rules.

RECORD-KEEPING

Keep a diary specifically for the letting in which important dates can be identified and notes made about telephone conversations with tenants, visits to the property, repair instructions issued to contractors, etc. In addition, full details should be kept separately for rent payments, the issue of notices, electrical and gas safety inspections, and tenancy start and expiry dates. The more information you record, the easier it will be to maintain the tenancy and deal with any problems.

SUMMARY

- ◆ If tenants wish to reserve your property, consider creating a pre-tenancy agreement and agree any charges should they fail to proceed.
- ◆ Decide in advance the amount of surety deposit you intend collecting and the government-approved deposit protection scheme you intend adopting.
- ◆ Prepare a standing-order mandate for ongoing rent payments and inform utility companies of the occupier's liability to pay bills.
- ◆ Collect the deposit and follow the relevant scheme rules at commencement of tenancy. Be certain to provide the tenant with details of the scheme being used within 14 days of collecting the deposit sum.
- ◆ Collect the first rent payment.
- ◆ Complete the check-in procedure with your tenants and obtain signatures on the inventory and tenancy agreement.

CHAPTER TEN

Managing the Tenancy

In this chapter:

◆ repairing obligations
◆ inspections
◆ harassment and illegal eviction
◆ managing late rent and arrears.

Scottish-born American author, Amelia E. Barr, wrote:

> *Events that are predestined require but little management. They manage themselves. They slip into place while we sleep, and suddenly we are aware that the thing we fear to attempt, is already accomplished.*

Some landlords believe they can leave their tenancies to progress to expiry without intervention. In reality, this premise results in being unprepared for the problems that can occur. Be aware of your responsibilities, plan ahead, equip yourself for difficulties that may arise, and your tenancy will be more fortuitous and less prone to calamity.

REPAIRING OBLIGATIONS

The Landlord and Tenant Act 1985 makes landlords responsible for most repairs of a dwelling let for less than seven years. This is **statute law** and cannot be undermined by contrary terms entered in a tenancy agreement. The Act means that you will usually have to undertake repairs, when required, to:

◆ the structure and exterior of the dwelling
◆ basins, sinks, baths, and other sanitary installations
◆ systems and appliances for providing hot water and heating.

Whilst the law is not conclusive, it is generally accepted that landlords are responsible for repairs to furniture and other appliances and equipment supplied by them. Liability should be clearly identified in the tenancy agreement for all other necessary repairs. Landlords are usually only required to **make good**, not to **improve**. A tenant recently lost his case in court because he was seeking satisfaction from a landlord who refused to install a damp-proof course to solve a problem of dampness. He lost because it was deemed the installation would be an improvement rather than a repair to something that already existed. If the landlord had refused to make good a faulty damp-proof course, the tenant would probably have won.

Tenants also have responsibilities. They must, for example, turn the water off to prevent damage if a leak occurs and guard against pipes freezing if going on holiday during winter. They should care for the dwelling and not wilfully or negligently damage it and ensure their guests and co-occupiers are equally mindful.

Prudent landlords will plan for all eventualities and have telephone numbers available of favoured electricians, plumbers and builders to remedy defects promptly.

INSPECTIONS

There is no formal requirement obliging landlords to conduct inspections during the tenancy; but there are numerous advantages to it. Landlords can:

- ◆ assess whether the property is being kept properly
- ◆ identify any repairs that are required
- ◆ identify new occupiers not recognised as tenants
- ◆ assess the tenant's intentions before expiry of the term.

Quarterly inspections on a mutually convenient date should be agreed, in advance, and confirmed in writing. A brief examination of each room and any garden area should be conducted and notes made regarding cleanliness and upkeep. Assuming you have no objection, ask the tenant whether they would like to continue occupying the property after the term has expired. Their answer will allow you to plan ahead and, where appropriate, issue notice at the required time (see Chapter 11).

Some tenants may prevent or impede you from undertaking inspections. They may have forgotten about the appointment, be irritated by the inconvenience or feel acrimonious towards you over another matter. In these circumstances, be acquiescent rather than mulish. Achieving an amicable compromise is likely to get you into the property and cause less problems, whereas a display of stubborn authoritarianism will just exacerbate any difficulties. If the tenant remains intractable, you can issue written notice (minimum of 24 hours) that you will gain access during a reasonable time of day to conduct the inspection. Always confirm that suitable provision exists in the tenancy agreement before employing this right.

HARASSMENT AND ILLEGAL EVICTION

Severe penalties can be applied to any landlord who illegally evicts or harasses their tenant (Protection from Eviction Act 1977). Be extremely careful not to cause either occurrence and be aware that unscrupulous tenants have been known to manipulate incidents purely for compensatory gain. Both statute and common law provide tenants with the right to **quiet enjoyment** of the dwelling. Any disturbance by the landlord may be construed as interfering with this right and give credence to a claim.

Examples of **harassment** might include:

♦ Using abusive or threatening language in verbal or written communications.
♦ Gaining access to the property without due notice, at unreasonable times of the day or night or for a purpose inconsistent with the terms of tenancy.
♦ Contacting the tenant's employer or bank regarding behaviour or rent arrears.
♦ Getting another person to encourage the tenant's payment of rent arrears.
♦ Any action that discourages the tenant's continued occupation or enjoyment of all or part of the dwelling, including interfering with or a withdrawal of services.

Examples of **illegal eviction** might include:

♦ Changing or adding locks on entrance doors without providing new keys.
♦ Undertaking work at the property that prevents occupation of it (unless an agreement has been reached permitting it).
♦ Terminating a tenancy without appropriate notice.
♦ Evicting a tenant without a court order.
♦ Turning off essential supplies such as water, gas or electricity, which forces the tenant to vacate.

MANAGING LATE RENT AND ARREARS

Rent is due by midnight on the day specified by the tenancy agreement or, when no date is indicated, the last day of the period. You must keep a record of all underpayments, late payments and non-payments of rent, as these can provide essential evidence if you later need to pursue possession of your property. Good record-keeping will also allow you to keep track of the tenant's account and identify the balance outstanding at any particular time. As soon as a payment is overdue, bring it to the tenant's attention by writing to them (keeping a copy for your files). If the tenancy involves a guarantor, send them a copy of the letter and remind them of their responsibility to meet any overdue amount.

There is no need to send any additional letters at this stage, even if the rent goes unpaid for the full duration of the period (weekly or monthly), but ensure you send one letter for *every* unpaid amount. The significance of maintaining accurate records and keeping written evidence of arrears will become clear when we examine how you go about obtaining possession in the next chapter.

Landlord's Action claims no one acts faster or more cost effectively than they do in dealing with bad tenants. They offer a fixed fee following three simple steps to ensure a positive outcome to such problems:

Step 1 costs £115. Within 48 hours of instruction a notice is served, in person, to the problem tenant. In six out of ten cases Landlord's Action claim this is the only action required. The tenant has 14 days to act. If they pay-up or leave, no further action is required. If they don't it's on to Step 2.

Step 2 costs £565. A solicitor approved by Landlord's Action issues proceedings. A court hearing date is set and a barrister instructed. He appears before a judge to obtain a possession order. If the tenant doesn't act on the court's order, it's on to Step 3.

Step 3 costs £198. Landlord's Action arrange for court bailiffs to remove the tenant and the vacant property is returned to the landlord for re-letting.

More information is available on Landlord Action's website at **www.landlordaction.co.uk**

An assured shorthold tenant may decide to purposely **withhold** rent because:

◆ a requested repair or replacement is outstanding;
◆ they have paid an expense they believe the landlord is liable for; or
◆ the end of tenancy has been reached and they have withheld the last month's rent in lieu of the deposit.

In each situation the rent remains lawfully due and this should be made clear to the tenant in writing. By withholding rent, they are breaking a fundamental obligation in the agreement and jeopardising their security of tenure as a result. However, under common law, the tenant can employ a procedure known as **set off** in certain circumstances. If a landlord is in breach of their repairing obligations, the tenant can obtain estimates and present them to the landlord. The tenant *must* advise the landlord that, if the work is not conducted within a set period, they intend to arrange it and pay the bill from rent due or owed.

If the landlord has started the process of seeking possession due to rent arrears, the tenant can set off arrears against repair costs *providing* the arrears are purely the result of the landlord's failure to deal with the repairs (i.e. arrears did not occur prior to the repairs becoming necessary).

SUMMARY

- Once a repair or replacement for which you are responsible is reported or identified, deal with it promptly.
- Undertake regular inspections of the property, giving advance written notice of at least 24 hours.
- Do not undertake any action which may be construed as harassment or illegal eviction.
- Keep adequate records of late or underpaid rent and arrears. Write to the tenant as soon as payment is overdue, reminding them of their obligations.

CHAPTER ELEVEN

End of Tenancy

In this chapter:

◆ planning for tenancy expiry
◆ issuing notice
◆ check-out
◆ dilapidations and deposit refund
◆ statutory periodic tenancy
◆ grounds for possession
◆ accelerated possession procedure.

An assured shorthold tenancy ends by notice, forfeiture or surrender (the latter being where *both* parties agree to early termination); or because it naturally expires at the end of the term. However, even though a tenancy has ended, the landlord cannot force their tenant to leave the premises. This is a golden rule of letting and landlords who disregard it do so at their peril.

PLANNING FOR TENANCY EXPIRY

At least *two months* prior to the end of the tenancy term, a landlord must assess what they and their tenant want to happen at expiry. If the tenant wishes to continue his occupation (and the landlord has no objection), the landlord can:

◆ create a new assured shorthold to commence following expiry of the current one (and with a new rent if desired); or
◆ allow the term to expire, in which case the tenancy would automatically continue as a **statutory periodic tenancy** with the same terms and conditions as the original. This type of tenancy runs according to the periodic nature of rent payments (usually month to month).

Alternatively, if the landlord wishes to bring the tenancy to an end at expiry of the current term, they must serve *at least two months'* notice (see below).

ISSUING NOTICE

If the landlord does *not* want a statutory periodic tenancy to be automatically created at the end of the term, they must serve due notice (according to the

Housing Act 1988) to their assured shorthold tenant. The tenant, on the other hand, does not normally have to serve notice to end their obligations and leave at the end of the term, unless the tenancy agreement makes it a requirement.

The form of notice is called **Section 21 – Notice Requiring Possession**. These can be obtained from a legal stationer (a version is also available online for £3.65 at **www.oyezformslink.co.uk**). Section 21 of the Housing Act 1988 describes the rules for notice issued **during the fixed term** and those for **after the fixed term has expired** (i.e. during a statutory periodic tenancy). We will deal here with the former only, Section 21(1)(b). To serve notice, you should complete the following procedure *exactly*:

1. Obtain a notice form.
2. Complete it with the details for tenant name (all joint tenants must be named on the notice), your own name and address, and the tenanted property address.
3. **Date possession is required by**: enter the last day of the tenancy term (this can in fact be for any time *at or after* expiry of the term *providing* the two-month rule below is followed *and* service is made within the tenancy term, including the last day of tenancy).
4a. **Date of notice**: enter the current date, *providing* it is *at least* two months before the date at 3 above (notice can be served at any time once the tenancy has begun, but it must always be at least two months prior to the possession date – but see 4b below); *and* providing you intend delivering it to the tenant(s) on the same day. If you intend posting the notice, add three days to the notice period to allow for delivery.
4b. If the tenancy rent periods are quarterly the minimum notice is three months; if six months or more, then six months' notice.
5. Sign the notice.
6. Make two copies of the completed notice for your files.
7. Serve the notice by hand or by post (ordinary first class post unless the tenancy agreement dictates something else). It is essential that you arrange for a witness when delivery is made in person. The courts accept that notice has been served if it has been delivered to the let property address (it does not have to be handed to the tenant in person).

Issuing notice in the correct format, with the correct dates and at the correct time are crucial elements to achieving vacant possession. Of the vast number of cases of possession taken to court by landlords and their agents, many are thrown out simply because documents have been inaccurately completed or wrongly issued. Whilst an experienced landlord with a meticulous eye for detail may wish to undertake this task under their own guidance, most would be wise to consider employing a solicitor or agent to complete it on their behalf.

The internet provides details of specialist agencies that will issue legal documents and deal with the process of tenant eviction on your behalf. They adopt a set price structure, which allows landlords acting independently to budget for such eventualities. In most cases, the administration is completed online and services offered range from issuing due notice to complete court possession case handling. Contact the following for further details, if this kind of service is of interest to you:

Landlord Action
Tel: 0870 389 0580
www.landlordaction.co.uk

Landlord Law
01603 763096
www.landlordlaw.co.uk

Regency Law
Tel: 01293 525665
www.tenancyeviction.org.uk

CHECK-OUT

On the last day of tenancy, after the tenant has removed their possessions and vacated, you should:

◆ Receive the keys and details of their forwarding address.

◆ Read gas, electricity and water meters, and inform all utility companies and the council-tax department that they have vacated (provide them with the tenant's new address for any final bills).

◆ Check that any telephone line has been disconnected.

◆ Turn water stop-taps, heating and hot water systems off and drain water tanks (if appropriate and according to the weather conditions).

◆ Inspect the property thoroughly for losses, damage and cleanliness, using the inventory for guidance (make notes and take photographs of any adverse observations).

◆ For security purposes, consider changing the locks and/or intruder alarm code.

◆ Install your 'To Let' boards and begin marketing for new tenants.

If the tenant fails to vacate on the last day of tenancy you will need to seek possession through the courts (see Grounds for Possession and Accelerated Possession Procedure).

DILAPIDATIONS AND DEPOSIT REFUND

Once the tenant has vacated and providing they have paid the rent in full, paid all utility bills they are liable for and have returned the property in a good condition (fair wear and tear excepted), the deposit protection scheme administrator should be instructed to return the tenant's deposit in accordance with the scheme's rules.

However, if damage or loss has occurred to the property or its contents – or if there are other tenancy agreement breaches that involve costs being incurred – you will need to draw up a dilapidation report and submit it to the tenant (within the time limits imposed by the relevant deposit protection scheme adopted).

If the tenant agrees the assessment of deposit deduction, the scheme administrator will distribute funds accordingly between landlord and tenant. If there is a disagreement, the relevant scheme operator will retain the amount disputed and the matter will then have to be settled by formal arbitration. Consult the scheme administrator as soon as possible, asking for details on how you should proceed in such cases.

When calculating the costs and expenses of property reinstatement, the landlord should:

◆ be fair and objective in their assessment and seek a second opinion where possible;

◆ obtain at least two and preferably three estimates for any repairs, purchases or services required;

◆ assess a deductible amount according to age and condition when replacing items damaged or lost;

◆ attach to the assessment of costs copies of any before and after photographic evidence;

◆ make sure you have a copy of the rules and regulations regarding the particular tenancy deposit protection scheme you have chosen to use. Follow the guidance offered and keep to the imposed timescales.

If you have followed earlier advice given in this book, the utility companies and council tax department should pursue the tenant over any unpaid bills. However, it is imperative you contact each authority to inform them when the tenant's liability ended and to provide them with the tenant's forwarding address, if known. If any authority attempts to pursue you for unpaid bills, refer them to the tenancy agreement and your tenancy commencement letter, which should clearly define the tenant has signed for liability during the period of tenancy.

If damage and other tenant liable expenses exceed the deposit amount, consider employing the Small Claims Court to recover the balance (after any dispute has been settled by the deposit protection scheme's arbitration service and assuming the exceeding sum is less than £5,000). Always check the tenant's obligations are clearly stated in the tenancy agreement and are relevant to the claim, before going to court.

STATUTORY PERIODIC TENANCY

A statutory periodic tenancy (SPT) arises if the landlord fails to intervene at the end of an assured shorthold tenancy (AST) *and* where the tenant stays in occupation. It is *automatic*; no additional documentation is required. The original terms and obligations of the AST continue as before. This arrangement can have advantages for the landlord and tenant because, as there is no fixed term, there is greater flexibility when either party wants the tenancy to end.

The landlord can terminate a SPT tenancy at any time by giving two months' written notice (but see below). The tenant has the same right, though their notice only needs to be one full rent period. To serve notice [Section 21(4)(a)], the landlord should follow the same procedure as before but with the following exception:

♦ A minimum of two months' notice (three months for quarterly rent payments; six months for six monthly rent payments) must be given *after* the AST has expired *and* with the expiry of notice being on the last day of a tenancy period. The tenancy period depends on the payment of rent. To calculate the date correctly (this is very important), you must refer to the original AST agreement. The SPT begins the day after the AST expires. So if it expires on 20 October, the SPT begins on 21 October. If the rent is monthly, then the last day of the first tenancy period in this example is 20 November, with subsequent periods also ending on 20th. Using this example, if you served notice on 5 November the tenancy would not end until 20 January.

It is easy to make mistakes when calculating notice dates, which is why I advised earlier in this book against using certain tenancy start dates or varying the rent collection day. Precision is important because errors can lead to unsuccessful possession proceedings if taken to court.

GROUNDS FOR POSSESSION

Although issuing notice, done correctly, will bring the AST or SPT to an end, it does not automatically give the landlord possession. Eviction requires a court order. If the tenancy term has ended, the landlord does not need to apply to court under any of the **grounds** set out below and can instead use the **accelerated possession procedure** (see later in this chapter).

However, to apply for a court order *during the tenancy term*, they must issue a (Section 8) Notice Seeking Possession and satisfy the court that they have a right to possession under one or more of the grounds. With AST tenants, landlords can only apply using Grounds 2, 8, 10 to 15 or 17, during the fixed term. This involves following a strict procedure and, in the case of discretionary grounds, success is not guaranteed. There are 17 grounds for possession falling into two distinct categories. They can be applied singularly or in combination:

◆ **Mandatory grounds** (1 to 8): the court *must* grant possession if the ground is proved by the landlord.
◆ **Discretionary grounds** (9 to 17): the court *may* grant possession if the ground is proved by the landlord.

The grounds for possession are:

(*Note*: Grounds 1 to 5 are *prior notice grounds* where the landlord must have issued notice to the tenant *before the tenancy began or at commencement*, that they may seek possession using that ground.)

Ground 1: The landlord lived in or intends to live in the property as their only or principal home.
Ground 2: The property is mortgaged and the lender wants possession (the loan must have started prior to the tenancy).
Ground 3: The tenancy fixed period is eight months or less and within 12 months of the tenancy starting it was let for a holiday.
Ground 4: The tenancy is a student-letting and within 12 months of the tenancy starting it was let to students by an educational establishment.
Ground 5: The property is held for use by a minister of religion and is now required for that purpose.
Ground 6: Substantial redevelopment of the property is intended which cannot be undertaken while the tenant is occupying it. This ground cannot be used if the property was purchased with an existing tenant.
Ground 7: The former tenant has died and no one has a right of succession to the tenancy.
Ground 8: The tenant owes at least two months' rent (if rent is paid monthly) or eight weeks' rent (if weekly), both when notice seeking possession is issued *and* at the time of the court hearing.
Ground 9: There is suitable alternative accommodation available (tenant's removal costs must be paid).

Ground 10: The tenant was behind with the rent when notice was served seeking possession *and* when court proceedings started.

Ground 11: The tenant has been persistently late in paying rent even though they were not behind with payments when possession proceedings began.

Ground 12: The tenant has broken one or more of the tenancy conditions (does not apply to rent payments).

Ground 13: The property has deteriorated due to the behaviour of the tenant or any other person living in it.

Ground 14: The tenant or someone visiting or living in the property has caused, or is likely to cause, a nuisance or annoyance to neighbours or anyone visiting the locality. Or they have been convicted of using the property or allowing it to be used for immoral or illegal purposes, or for an arrestable offence, committed in the property or locality.

Ground 15: The furniture has deteriorated because it has been ill-treated by the tenant or any other person living in the property.

Ground 16: The tenancy was given because the tenant was previously employed by you or a former landlord, but is no longer being employed.

Ground 17: The tenancy was granted based on a false statement knowingly or recklessly made by the tenant, or by someone acting at the tenant's instigation.

Notice must be given to the tenant *before* starting court proceedings. The 'Section 8' notice period varies according to the ground(s) being used:

◆ For Grounds 3, 4, 8, 10, 11, 12, 13, 15 or 17 at least two weeks' notice must be given.

◆ For Grounds 1, 2, 5, 6, 7, 9 and 16 at least two months' notice must be given. If the tenancy is a SPT, then the notice period must end on the last day of a period. In addition, the notice period must be at least as long as the tenancy period, for example three months in the case of rent being paid quarterly (but limited to six months for a yearly tenancy period).

◆ For Ground 14 there is no notice period. Court proceedings can start as soon as notice is issued.

Section 8 Notice forms can be obtained from legal stationers and on-line at **www.letlink.co.uk**, **www.landlordlaw.co.uk** or **www.legalhelpers.co.uk** The same rules apply for completing the form as for the Section 21 notice, except that you must enter the ground(s) under which possession is being sought and explain the circumstances why the ground is being cited. You must enter the wording of the ground *exactly* as it appears in the Housing Act (obtain copies of the 1988 and 1996 Acts from your local HMSO for reference). *Note*: the text descriptions above are *not* as written in the Acts; they have been condensed for easier understanding.

When notice is being issued because of rent arrears, a schedule of the arrears should accompany the notice *and* it must be in a format acceptable to the courts. The standard County Court process is often slow and bureaucratic and many landlords are reluctant to use it. As one small mistake can cost you the entire case, it is wise to consider employing a solicitor experienced in property matters to assist and guide you. If the tenant fails to remedy the breach or it is one that cannot be remedied, the landlord has 12 months in which to commence court proceedings for possession.

ACCELERATED POSSESSION PROCEDURE

The accelerated possession procedure (APP) was introduced to help streamline the process for landlords seeking possession of their property. Although it does not always live up to expectations, it is easier than the standard process. However, the APP cannot be used to recover rent arrears. For assured shorthold tenancies, the APP can only be used at the end of the fixed term or during a periodic tenancy *and* a Section 21 Notice must first have been issued. All the necessary forms and a set of guidance notes can be obtained from the County Court or on-line at **www.hmcourts-service.gov.uk**

The Accelerated Possession Procedure can be used when claiming possession at the end of the initial contracted period known as the 'Shorthold Term', which is when the tenancy term-certain of an Assured Shorthold expires but the tenant fails to vacate; and/or when using mandatory possession on grounds 1, 3, 4 and/or 5.

Remember that, even after successfully obtaining a possession order from the court, the tenant *still* cannot be evicted by his landlord. The landlord must first seek a warrant from the court. The court will then arrange for bailiffs to perform the eviction. Taking defaulting tenants to court is usually best avoided, if at all possible, but the APP provides a fast-track legal solution for those situations that demand it.

SUMMARY

◆ Issue notice at the appropriate time to bring the assured shorthold tenancy to an end, unless you want a statutory periodic tenancy to arise automatically.

◆ Choose the Section 21 Notice route, when seeking possession, in preference to the more protracted Section 8 Notice method.

◆ Assess dilapidations fairly and objectively at the end of tenancy and return the tenant's deposit (or balance of) as quickly as possible.

◆ Avoid going to court unless absolutely necessary but, if there is no alternative and circumstances are appropriate, consider using the Accelerated Possession Procedure to regain possession.

◆ Get help and advice from landlords who have experience of using the court service or consider employing a solicitor to assist you when undertaking legal action to recover your property.

CHAPTER TWELVE

Letting in Scotland

In this chapter:

- ◆ legislation affecting Scottish landlords
- ◆ short assured tenancy
- ◆ the deposit
- ◆ safety inspections
- ◆ extending the tenancy
- ◆ ending a short assured tenancy
- ◆ seeking possession
- ◆ houses in multiple occupation
- ◆ further information.

Landlords letting property in Scotland are governed by laws and regulations that vary from those for England and Wales. Whilst the main principles and framework are similar, there are fundamental differences of which landlords should be aware. These include:

LANDLORD REGISTRATION

From March 2006, **all landlords** letting one or more properties in the private rented sector in Scotland must have applied for registration or be registered. This is the law, regardless of whether the landlord lives in Scotland or not. Provisions for the creation of a national Register of Landlords was introduced as part of the Anti-Social Behaviour Bill, which was passed through the Scottish Parliament late in 2004. The main exceptions to registration are if you are a landlord letting part of your own home or the letting is to a tenant of an agricultural holding or croft. Holiday lets are also exempt. Failure to comply is a criminal offence that attracts severe penalties. These include fines up to £5,000. In cases where the Sheriff serves a rent penalty notice on a landlord who has been letting a house without registration, tenants of that house will not be required to pay rent until the notice is revoked or overturned on appeal.

Landlords can apply to register online at **www.landlordregistrationscotland. gov.uk** or through their local authority. On applying, they must provide certain mandatory information about themselves and their properties. Landlords must pay a fee to become registered and the amount varies throughout Scotland, because the principal part of the fee structure takes individual local authority costs into account. Landlords with several properties in multiple areas must register with each local authority. Registration lasts three years and after this period landlords must renew their entry on the register to operate legally.

More advice and information about registration is available at the following websites:

www.betterrentingscotland.com
www.scottishlandlords.com

Or contact the local authority where your let property is situated.

LEGISLATION AFFECTING SCOTTISH LANDLORDS

Most new tenancies created after 2 January 1989 are governed by Part II of the Housing (Scotland) Act 1988. It introduced **assured** tenancies which are similar in design to those for England and Wales. There are, however, critical differences in the way these tenancies are named, established, managed and terminated. The Housing (Scotland) Act 2001 introduced some changes in definition, particularly relating to disability and discrimination, but the Scottish Executive have confirmed these have not altered significantly the aspects of tenancy introduced by the 1988 Act.

New legislation from 2007

The Housing (Scotland) Act 2006 introduces a new 'repairing standard' for private rented accommodation and supplies important new rights for tenants who need to get repairs carried out because their homes don't reach this standard. Under this new law, if the landlord fails to carry out essential repairs, tenants will be able to take their case to a private rented housing committee (PRHC). The PRHC will have the power to order the landlord to do the repairs, if necessary. The new powers are due to come into force in Scotland towards the end of 2007 – for more information visit **www.scotland.shelter.org.uk/advice/advice-6308.cfm**

SHORT ASSURED TENANCY

A **short assured tenancy** (SAT) is comparable with the '**assured shorthold tenancy**' in England and Wales. There are two major disparities:

◆ The landlord must give to the tenant, *before* any agreement is signed, a notice (called AT5) that the tenancy being proposed is to be a SAT. If notice is not properly issued, the resulting tenancy will be the **assured** type, affording the tenant far greater security of tenure than was probably intended. The notice can be obtained from a law stationer or free from **www.clickdocs.co.uk** or **www.scotland.gov.uk/housing/leaflets/at5-00.asp** (a copy is also provided for reference under the Appendix at the back of this book).

◆ The tenancy must be for a minimum fixed term of six months.

The tenancy agreement *must* be in writing and a copy has to be given to the tenant. There is no scope for a verbal agreement and landlords are unable to charge a fee for providing the document. If a tenant is not given a written agreement or receives one that does not reflect the terms of tenancy, they can ask the Sheriff to have one drawn up or apply for a revision of existing terms.

THE DEPOSIT

In Scotland, landlords cannot demand more than a sum equal to two months' rent as a surety deposit. In addition, it is generally forbidden to ask for a premium or key-money in granting, renewing, continuing or assigning an assured or short assured tenancy and a fine of up to £400 is applicable to those that do.

As this book goes to press there are proposals being discussed by Scottish ministers which could reform and regulate how tenancy deposits are taken and managed. One suggestion is to duplicate the provisions introduced in England and Wales (Housing Act 2004), though ministers would like first to assess whether mandatory registration has a positive impact on rogue landlords, thereby making the regulation of deposits unnecessary. The Scottish Executive announced an amendment to the Housing Bill (Scotland) late in 2005, which allows new powers to be introduced through the Housing (Scotland) Act 2006. New regulations could deal with disputes over dilapidation amounts and provide an alternative resolution procedure, preventing a need for either the landlord or the tenant to go to court. Other measures could speed up the process of landlords refunding deposits to their tenants. Provisions in the Act come into force in stages from March 2007 and the Scottish Executive has stated it will make further announcements as the year progresses. For more information, consult the Scottish Executive's website at **www.scotland.gov.uk** or telephone the Scottish Association of Landlords on 0131 270 4774.

SAFETY INSPECTIONS

The regulations for electrical and gas safety, and for furnishings, are the same as those outlined previously for England and Wales.

EXTENDING THE TENANCY

SATs can continue beyond the expiry date of the first term. Providing neither the landlord nor the tenant intervene (that is, they do nothing at all at expiry of the initial term), the new period of tenancy will begin automatically and this will be the same length as the first period (subject to the new term being either the lesser of the term or one year). This subsequent period is called a **continued short assured tenancy** (CSAT).

Alternatively, the landlord can create a new SAT, provided that the tenant agrees and the property and parties remain the same. The new SAT is not subject to the same set-up procedure as the original. There is no requirement to serve a new AT5 notice and there is no minimum term.

ENDING A SHORT ASSURED TENANCY

The landlord must issue a **notice to quit**. The period of notice depends on the nature of rent payments, that is, the periodic structure of the tenancy. If the property is let:

◆ weekly, fortnightly or monthly, then at least four weeks' notice must be given; or
◆ quarterly, then at least 31 days' notice must be given (one third of the tenancy period or 40 days whichever is the lesser); or
◆ yearly, then at least 40 days' notice must be given.

Notice cannot take effect earlier than the expiry date of the agreement and must contain prescribed information for the tenant in accordance with the Housing Act, otherwise it will be invalid. Issuing a notice to quit is appropriate prior to granting the tenant a new SAT or as a first step to seeking possession. It brings the current tenancy to an end (at expiry of the term), but it does not mean the tenant has to leave the property. As with letting in England and Wales, a tenant cannot be evicted without a court order.

SEEKING POSSESSION

To seek possession, landlords must issue formal notice (*Form AT6: Notice of Proceedings*). For SATs, notice does not need to be submitted on an AT6 form, though it can be used, but must contain the **grounds** specified in the Housing (Scotland) Act 1988 through which possession is being sought. The **Notice to quit** and the **Notice of proceedings** can be issued together, subject to the minimum notice periods. The minimum notice period when seeking possession under grounds 1, 2, 5, 6, 7, 9 or 17 is two months. For any other ground, it is two weeks (but be aware that the Notice to quit has a minimum of 28 days).

A 'Notice to quit' is **not** required if the landlord is seeking possession **during the term** of the lease due to a breach by the tenant.

The Grounds for Possession are almost identical to those described in Chapter 11 except:

- ◆ **Ground 8**: the tenant must be in *three months* arrears of rent when the notice of proceedings is served and at the date of the hearing.
- ◆ **Ground 10**: the *tenant* has given the landlord a Notice to Quit, which has expired, but has continued to occupy the property. The landlord can use this ground providing they seek an order for possession within six months of the notice expiring.
- ◆ **Ground 12**: some rent remains outstanding at the beginning of court proceedings *and* at the time Notice of Proceedings is served.
- ◆ **Ground 13**: the tenant has broken one or more obligations of tenancy other than any involving the payment of rent.
- ◆ **Ground 14**: as Ground 13 of the Housing Act 1988 for England and Wales.
- ◆ **Ground 15**: as Ground 14 of the Housing Act 1988 for England and Wales.
- ◆ **Ground 16**: as Ground 15 of the Housing Act 1988 for England and Wales.
- ◆ **Ground 17**: as Ground 16 of the Housing Act 1988 for England and Wales.

There is no equivalent ground under Scottish law for a private sector landlord to seek possession because a tenancy was granted based on false statements made by a tenant. In addition, there is no equivalent fast-track method of regaining possession in Scotland, unlike the Accelerated Possession Procedure available in England and Wales. Landlords are advised to obtain the exact wording of the grounds in the Housing (Scotland) Act 1988 when quoting them for possession purposes. Always remember that a tenant cannot be evicted unless an Order for Possession has been granted by the Sheriff.

HOUSES IN MULTIPLE OCCUPATION (HiMOs)

HiMO landlords tend to be dealt with punitively under Scottish law. It is a harsh, complex and bureaucratic regime. By tightening the definition of what constitutes a HiMO and by inflicting strict regulations through local authority imposed minimum standards, the Scottish Parliament stated its intention to *'get rid of slum landlords!'*. Although this will undoubtedly be one of the results, it has also increased the supply and maintenance costs for HiMO landlords.

On 1 October 2000, a compulsory licensing scheme was introduced for all HiMO landlords ['Civic Government (Scotland) Act (Licensing of Houses in Multiple Occupation) Order 2000']. The scheme was introduced gradually over three years, so a property shared by two or more unrelated people, let after 1 October 2003, is likely to be classed as a HiMO. Local authorities were granted powers to impose standards, which differ from one authority to another, about the condition of the building and how it is managed. The exemptions include registered homes, residential care homes, private hospitals and residential accommodation for school students.

HiMO landlords will also be further affected by measures introduced by the Housing Act (Scotland) 2006. Although HiMO landlords will already have been found to be 'fit and proper' by the local authority and will have paid for a licence, their name(s) will still need to be placed on the 'Register of Landlords'. Guidance suggests this will happen automatically. There will be no requirement to apply or pay again, unless the landlord owns other properties that are not HiMOs. Where there are joint-owners **each** joint-owner must apply (one of the joint-owners in the same family is entitled to a discount of the standard fee).

Landlords concerned about HiMOs and licensing should consult the local authority (where their property is situated) for further information and advice *before* creating a tenancy.

FURTHER INFORMATION

Paper copies of relevant legislation, such as The Housing (Scotland) Acts, can be obtained from a local TSO (The Stationery Office) or viewed online at **www.opsi.gov.uk**

Tenancy documents and notices can be obtained from a law stationer. There are also versions available on the internet, for example **www.clickdocs.co.uk/ housing-documents-scotland.htm** offer sample agreements for about £30.

There are multiple internet links for legal information about renting in Scotland at **www.scottishlaw.org.uk**

The Scottish Executive provides information and free leaflets useful to landlords. These can be viewed on-line at **www.scotland.gov.uk/housing/leaflets** or by contacting them at:

Scottish Executive Development Department
Victoria Quay
Edinburgh EH6 6QQ
Tel: 08457 741 741

Other valuable information is available from:

Better Renting Scotland
(created by The Scottish Executive)
Website: **www.betterrentingscotland.com**

Citizens Advice Scotland
Spectrum House
2 Powderhall Road
Edinburgh EH7 4GB
Tel: 0131 550 1000
Website: **www.cas.org.uk**

Scottish Association of Landlords
20 Forth Street
Edinburgh
EH1 3LH
Tel: 0131 270 4774
Website: **www.scottishlandlords.com**

SUMMARY

◆ Be aware of the different legislation affecting landlords in Scotland.
◆ To create a short assured tenancy you must issue an AT5 Notice to the tenant before signing the agreement.
◆ To prevent a continued short assured tenancy being automatically created, with the same length of term as the original, you must issue a Notice to Quit at the appropriate time prior to expiry of the short assured term.
◆ Houses in multiple occupation are subject to a strict licensing scheme. Landlords should be aware of the HiMO definition, enforced minimum standards, and other regulations affecting them, before starting a tenancy.
◆ Be aware the Housing (Scotland) Act 2006 introduced a mandatory registration regime for **all** landlords operating in the private rented sector in Scotland.

CHAPTER THIRTEEN

Troubleshooting

In this chapter:

- ◆ absentee tenants
- ◆ neighbour disputes
- ◆ succession by husband or wife
- ◆ landlords living outside the UK
- ◆ receiving/sending documents by fax and e-mail
- ◆ under-18s.

This section explains some of the most common predicaments faced by landlords.

ABSENTEE TENANTS

There is nothing more frustrating than a tenant in arrears of rent and *apparently* absent from the property. The landlord is faced with a dilemma: *has the tenant vacated permanently or do they intend to return?* It may be that they are:

- ◆ on holiday
- ◆ in hospital
- ◆ visiting friends
- ◆ working away from home or
- ◆ in prison.

Taking possession of the property, changing locks or re-letting it to alternative tenants may result in alarming and expensive consequences should the absent tenant return. Any action preventing the tenant's access to or occupation of the dwelling, without a court order, is likely to be a breach of the Protection from Eviction Act 1977. *There is no maximum fine* for such an offence. There are actions landlords can take, but these should be done quickly and thoroughly to corroborate suspicions:

1. Issue written 24 hours notice of your intention to inspect the property and keep a copy for your files. Hand-deliver this through the letter-box of the property with a witness.

2. At inspection, look for irrefutable evidence that the tenant has moved out. Are any of their possessions still in the property? Is there food in the kitchen? Is mail stacked behind the door?

3. Try to contact the tenant at their place of work or through relatives and friends whose details were given at application. If you succeed in making contact and the tenant confirms they no longer wish to live in the dwelling, ask for their voluntary **surrender of tenancy** in writing.

4. Talk to neighbours and ask when they last saw or spoke to the tenant.

5. Gather as much information as possible and maintain a diary of the times you called at the property or attempted to contact the tenant by telephone.

If, despite your efforts, there remains even the slightest doubt that the tenant may return to reclaim occupation:

6. Issue formal notice to bring the tenancy to an end, if applicable, and/or seek possession through the courts using the accelerated possession procedure (the accelerated possession procedure can only be used to regain possession at the end of the assured shorthold fixed term). Possession can be sought during the fixed term, subject to one or more of the 'grounds for possession' applying, but the case needs to be taken to the appropriate local county court using the standard procedure.

Legalhelpers stock a notice for landlords who find they have tenants' goods remaining in an apparently abandoned property. This is particularly useful where tenants are untraceable or simply do not wish to collect their possessions. The notice provides the landlord with a legal means of selling the goods. If the tenant later comes to collect them (after notice has been served), the landlord must pay them the amount received and this must be a reasonable price. However, expenses incurred for moving and disposal can be deducted. The notice must provide at least 28 days for the tenant to collect the goods, but if there are outstanding disputes and debts owed by the tenant (prior to the issue of notice), the notice period must be at least three months. Any legal action involved with the goods must be resolved prior to notice being issued. The notice costs £20. For more information contact Legalhelpers on 0870 321 9865 or order by post at Legalhelpers Ltd, Freepost MID23567, Stoke-on-Trent ST1 5BR or visit their website at: **www.legalhelpers.co.uk**

NEIGHBOUR DISPUTES

If neighbours complain about the behaviour of your tenant:

♦ Obtain the complaint in writing.

♦ Get both sides of the argument and assess the validity of complaint.

- Write to the tenant and explain their obligations under the tenancy agreement.
- Provide a 'cooling off' period to see whether matters improve.
- Ask the local authority if they offer a mediation service for neighbours in dispute and, where excessive noise is being caused, consult the environmental health department.
- If all else fails, consider issuing notice to bring a statutory periodic tenancy to an end or seek possession through the courts via grounds 12 and 14 (discretionary) for assured shorthold tenancies during the fixed term.

SUCCESSION BY HUSBAND OR WIFE

When couples have a joint tenancy and one decides to vacate, the status of each party is unchanged under the terms of the agreement. Both remain equally liable to pay the rent. Sometimes an amicable arrangement will be made between the parties and the landlord which brings the former tenancy to an end (by mutually agreeing 'surrender'), allowing the remaining partner to continue occupation under a new tenancy.

However, congenial determinations are not always so easy to achieve. They are particularly problematic in matters regarding separation and divorce or the death of one partner *and* where the tenancy is not jointly held. The landlord must consider carefully what **succession** rights apply to the remaining or surviving partner (if not the original tenant). Above all else, they must ensure they do not inadvertently harass or illegally evict the individual by misunderstanding their status and legal entitlement.

If it is a statutory periodic tenancy and the tenant dies, the surviving spouse, or anyone who was living with the tenant as husband or wife, has an automatic right to succeed to the tenancy. There can, however, only be one succession in this instance. If the surviving spouse dies, the tenancy ends. However, during an assured shorthold tenancy, the executors of the deceased's estate will decide whether anyone has a claim to the tenancy.

Matters involving separation and divorce are dealt with in a slightly different manner. In some circumstances, the Family Law Act 1996 provides limited security of tenure for the partner or cohabitee when the tenant-partner has vacated the property. An **occupation order** or **order of transfer** is usually made during matrimonial court proceedings and landlords are advised to deal direct with the remaining partner's appointed solicitor, to obtain appropriate information.

The Civil Partnership Act 2004 extended many legal entitlements to those of the same sex which were once exclusively enjoyed by married couples. Whilst the rights to succession and assignment are greater for the surviving or separated partner living in a council house or housing association property, there are circumstances where equal rights are now granted to civil partners renting from a private sector landlord.

LANDLORDS LIVING OUTSIDE THE UNITED KINGDOM

Many people choose to leave the UK to live, work or retire abroad. This applies to landlords too, but they must make special provisions for their tenants and inform the Inland Revenue before doing so. The usual arrangement is for an agent to be appointed who will collect and distribute rent and deal with day-to-day management issues. Landlords living abroad should be aware that:

◆ Tenants have a legal right to the name and address of their landlord, regardless of where they are residing.

◆ When employing the Accelerated Possession Procedure, agents cannot sign the form N5B on behalf of the non-resident landlord (a solicitor will need to be appointed to represent them instead).

◆ Unless a landlord has applied for and received an 'exemption certificate' from the HM Revenue & Customs' Centre for Non-Residents (CNR) or the rent payable is less than £100 per week, the agent (or tenant if rent is paid direct to the landlord) will normally be responsible for deducting the landlord's tax from the rent. There are, in addition, routine forms to complete and annual reports have to be submitted. For full details about the 'Non-Resident Landlords Scheme', contact CNR on 0845 070 0040 or visit the website at **www.hmrc.gov.uk**

RECEIVING/SENDING DOCUMENTS BY FAX AND E-MAIL

Most written material sent by fax or e-mail can be held as legal evidence in a court of law. There are countless examples on public record. Precedent was probably set in the 1980s by the Oliver North, Iran/contra affair, where electronic mail was accepted as admissible evidence in court. As the use of this medium became more widespread, the UK legal system had to consider and acknowledge the validity of cyber-text and make judgment on what constitutes a signature. Various Acts of Parliament have since cited the electronic medium and confirmed it as an applicable form of *legal* communication.

When sending or receiving anything by fax or e-mail consider the following:

◆ Tenancy documents and notices that are required to be in **prescribed form** must correspond with the criteria laid down in the Housing Act 1988 (as amended by the Housing Act 1996). This means that they must have a particular layout or include predetermined phrases to be legitimate.

- The Electronic Communications Act 2000 makes digital signatures legally binding in most circumstances. The signature does not necessarily have to be handwritten. It can be typed, but it should be certified by the author as originating from him or her and be issued with legal intent.
- The Defamation Act 1996 makes it an offence to disseminate defamatory statements. Phrases acceptable to you may be interpreted as being offensive by someone else. In addition, as e-mails can be submitted to court as evidence, statements issued may also be misconstrued as harassment (see Chapter 10).

UNDER-18s

The law does not prevent a landlord letting their property to someone under the age of 18. However, a **minor** cannot be bound by contract and difficulties may therefore arise if there is a breach of the tenancy terms. For example, a tenant aged 17 may be obliged to pay rent but, if they fail to do so, the landlord cannot seek satisfaction through the courts as they could with someone aged 18 or over.

Although this dilemma is probably best avoided, it *can* be resolved by securing a guarantor (see Chapter 7). The application of a watertight Guarantor Agreement is essential in this situation and a solicitor will be able to assist in devising one pertinent to your needs. Guarantors should be fully referenced and made liable for all of the tenant's obligations should default occur.

Appendix 1

EXAMPLE OF FORM AT5 (SCOTLAND)

HOUSING (SCOTLAND) ACT 1988

NOTICE UNDER SECTION 32 TO BE
SERVED ON A PROSPECTIVE TENANT
OF A SHORT ASSURED TENANCY

ASSURED TENANCIES   AT5

HOUSING (SCOTLAND) ACT 1988

NOTICE UNDER SECTION 32 TO BE SERVED ON A PROSPECTIVE TENANT OF A SHORT ASSURED TENANCY

IMPORTANT: INFORMATION FOR PROSPECTIVE TENANT(S)

This notice informs you as prospective tenant(s) that the tenancy being offered by the prospective landlord(s) is a short assured tenancy under Section 32 of the Housing (Scotland) Act 1988.

Please read this notice carefully.

Part 1 To   (name of prospective tenant(s))

NOTE 1 TO PROSPECTIVE TENANT.

TO BE VALID THIS NOTICE MUST BE SERVED BEFORE THE CREATION OF A TENANCY AGREEMENT. A SHORT ASSURED TENANCY WILL NOT EXIST IF A VALID NOTICE HAS NOT BEEN SERVED.

Part 2 I your prospective landlord(s)/I your prospective landlord's agent*

(name of landlord(s))

of

(address and telephone number of landlord(s))

give notice that the tenancy being offered to you of the house at

(address of house)

*delete as appropriate

to which this notice relates is to be a short assured tenancy in terms of Section 32 of the Housing (Scotland) Act 1988.

Signed

(landlord(s) or landlord's agent)

Date

NOTE 2 TO PROSPECTIVE TENANT.

A SHORT ASSURED TENANCY IS A SPECIAL FORM OF TENANCY. UNLESS IT FOLLOWS IMMEDIATELY AFTER ANOTHER SHORT ASSURED TENANCY OF THE SAME HOUSE, (WITH THE SAME TENANT) IT MUST BE FOR NOT LESS THAN 6 MONTHS.

NOTE 3 TO PROSPECTIVE TENANT.

A LANDLORD OF A SHORT ASSURED TENANCY HAS SPECIAL RIGHTS TO REPOSSESS THE HOUSE. IF THE LANDLORD TERMINATES THE TENANCY BY ISSUING A VALID NOTICE TO QUIT AND GIVES THE TENANT AT LEAST 2 MONTHS NOTICE (OR A LONGER PERIOD IF THE TENANCY AGREEMENT PROVIDES) OF HIS INTENTION TO REPOSSESS THE HOUSE THE COURT MUST GRANT THE LANDLORD AN ORDER ALLOWING HIM TO EVICT THE TENANT IF HE APPLIES FOR ONE AT THE END OF THE TENANCY PERIOD SET OUT IN THE TENANCY AGREEMENT.

Part 3. Address and telephone number of agent if appropriate:

of landlord(s) agent

of tenant's (s) agent

NOTE 4 TO PROSPECTIVE TENANT.

A TENANT OF A SHORT ASSURED TENANCY HAS A SPECIAL RIGHT TO APPLY TO A RENT ASSESSMENT COMMITTEE FOR A RENT DETERMI-NATION FOR THE TENANCY.

NOTE 5 TO PROSPECTIVE TENANT.

IF YOU AGREE TO TAKE UP THE TENANCY AFTER YOUR LANDLORD HAS SERVED THIS NOTICE ON YOU YOUR TENANCY WILL BE A SHORT ASSURED TENANCY. YOU SHOULD KEEP THIS NOTICE IN A SAFE PLACE ALONG WITH THE WRITTEN DOCUMENT SETTING OUT THE TERMS OF TENANCY WHICH YOUR LANDLORD MUST PROVIDE UNDER SECTION 30 OF THE HOUSING (SCOTLAND) ACT 1988 ONCE THE TERMS ARE AGREED.

NOTE 6 TO PROSPECTIVE TENANT.

IF YOU REQUIRE FURTHER GUIDANCE ON ASSURED AND SHORT AS-SURED TENANCIES, CONSULT A SOLICITOR OR ANY ORGANISATION WHICH GIVES ADVICE ON HOUSING MATTERS.

SPECIAL NOTES FOR EXISTING TENANTS
1. If you already have a regulated tenancy, other than a short tenancy, should you give it up and take a new tenancy in the same house or another house owned by the same landlord, that tenancy cannot be an assured tenancy or a short assured tenancy. Your tenancy will continue to be a regulated tenancy.

2. If you have a short tenancy under the Tenant's Rights etc. (Scotland) Act 1980 of the Rent (Scotland) Act 1984 your landlord can offer you an assured tenancy or short assured tenancy of the same or another house on the expiry of your existing tenancy.

3. If you are an existing tenant and are uncertain about accepting the proposed short assured tenancy you are strongly advised to consult a solicitor or any organisation which gives advice on housing matters.

ASSURED TENANCIES

HOUSING (SCOTLAND) ACT 1988

NOTES FOR LANDLORDS TO BE READ WITH NOTICE AT5.
THESE NOTES ARE FOR GUIDANCE ONLY AND ARE NOT A DEFINITIVE
INTERPRETATION OF THE LAW

WHEN TO USE THIS NOTICE
1. You should use this notice only when you wish to inform a prospective tenant or tenants that the tenancy being offered by you is a short assured tenancy under Section 32 of the Housing (Scotland) Act 1988.

2. You must serve the notice on the prospective tenant or tenants before the creation of any tenancy agreement. If it is not served before the creation of the tenancy agreement the tenancy will not be a short assured tenancy.

ABOUT SHORT ASSURED TENANCIES

3. A short assured tenancy is a special form of assured tenancy which in the first instance must be for not less than 6 months. It gives you special rights to repossess the house (see paragraph 4) and special rights for tenants to apply to a Rent Assessment Committee for a rent determination (see paragraphs 5 and 6).

Repossession of the Property
4. As landlord, if you obtain a possession order from the Sheriff, you may repossess the house you are letting on the short assured tenancy. Before applying for a possession order you must:

4.1 Issue a valid Notice to Quit to terminate the tenancy at its expiry date, and not offer your tenant another tenancy.

4.2 Give your tenant notice of your intention to apply for the order. The notice must be for at least 2 months unless your tenancy agreement provides for a longer period. If you fulfil these 2 conditions the Sheriff must grant you the order.

Rent
5. Unless a rent for the tenancy has already been determined by a Rent Assessment Committee, a tenant of a short assured tenancy has a right to seek a rent determination from a Rent Assessment Committee at any time during the tenancy. On receiving an application, the Committee will consider if it is appropriate to determine a market rent.

6. The Rent Assessment Committee will make a rent determination only if it considers there is a sufficient number of similar houses in the locality let on assured tenancies and the rent payable for the tenancy is significantly higher than the landlord might reasonably expect to charge having regard to rent levels for those tenancies. A rent determination made by the Committee will be the maximum payable for the tenancy from the date specified.

HOW TO USE THIS NOTICE
7. Before you and your prospective tenant make a binding agreement to let a house, you should complete Parts 1, 2 and 3 of the Notice. The Notice should then be given or sent to the prospective tenant or tenants. The tenancy will be a short assured tenancy as long as you have fulfilled all your requirements. The tenant should keep the Notice with the written document setting out the terms of the tenancy which have been agreed, and which must be provided by a landlord under Section 30 of the Housing (Scotland) Act 1988. You are also advised to keep a copy of Notice AT5 for your own records.

FURTHER GUIDANCE
8. If you are uncertain about the question of tenancy status or uncertain about how to complete this Notice, you should consult a solicitor or any organisation which gives advice on housing matters.

9. Further guidance on assured and short tenancies is available in "Assured Tenancies in Scotland – A Guide for Landlords and Tenants". Copies can be obtained from any office of the Rent Assessment Panel, Citizens Advice Bureau, Housing Advisory Centre or from any office of the Rent Registration Service.

Appendix 2

EXAMPLE OF:

**PROFESSIONAL TENANT REFERENCE
APPLICATION FORM**

SUPPLIED BY
FORLANDLORDS.CO.UK

ForLandlords.co.uk

Becor House, Green Lane, Lincoln LN6 7DL
T 0870 703 9009

The **online resource** ForLandlords

Tenant information

1. Tenant details   This section should be completed by the **Tenant**

Title: [   ]   First name: [   ]   Initials: [   ]   Surname: [   ]

Other name(s): [   ]   Date of birth: [   ]

2. Current address of the prospective tenant   This section should be completed by the **Tenant**

[   ]

[   ]   Post code [ ][ ][ ][ ][ ][ ]

Period at address: [   ] years [   ] months   Email: [   ]

Telephone: [   ]   Mobile: [   ]

Property owner ☐   Council tenant ☐   Private tenant ☐   Living with parents/relatives ☐

Have you any County Court Judgments, court decrees, bankruptcy or administration orders?   Yes ☐ No ☐

If yes, please detail on a separate sheet.

3. Previous addresses of the prospective tenant   This section should be completed by the **Tenant**

Where have you been living during the last 3 years?
Please provide previous address(es) and dates of residency (over 3 months), attaching a separate sheet if necessary.

Address 2 [   ]

[   ]   Post code [ ][ ][ ][ ][ ][ ]

Period at address: [   ] years [   ] months

Address 3 [   ]

[   ]   Post code [ ][ ][ ][ ][ ][ ]

Period at address: [   ] years [   ] months

4. Current estate agent/solicitor/managing agent/landlord   This section should be completed by the **Tenant**

Name of estate agent/solicitor/managing agent/landlord (delete as appropriate) [   ]

Address [   ]

[   ]   Post code [ ][ ][ ][ ][ ][ ]

Tel (day): [   ]   Tel (evening): [   ]

Fax: [   ]   Email: [   ]

Page no.: **1 of 3**

Becor House, Green Lane, Lincoln LN6 7DL
T 0870 703 9009 F 0870 751 5552

The **online resource** For**Landlords**

5. Tenant's employment status
This section should be completed by the **Tenant**

Employed ☐   Self employed ☐   On contract ☐   Retired ☐

Unemployed ☐   Student ☐   Independent means ☐   Proof is required if you tick this box.

Details of current employer/pension administrator/accountant/auditor/solicitor (delete as appropriate)

Company name [   ]   Contact name/position [   ]

Address [   ]

[   ]   Post code [   ][   ][   ][   ][   ][   ]

Tel: [   ]   Fax: [   ]

Email: [   ]

Gross salary/pension/drawings (delete as appropriate) £ [   ] per annum

Payroll/service/pension number [   ]

Position held: [   ]   Starting date in this position: [   ]

Is this position permanent? Yes ☐ No ☐

Will your employment change before the proposed tenancy starts? Yes ☐ No ☐ If yes, please detail on a separate sheet.

6. Tenant's previous employment / occupation
This section should be completed by the **Tenant**

If you have not worked in your current position for at least 18 months, please provide details of where you have previously worked, including dates of joining and leaving employment (attach a separate sheet if necessary).

Company name [   ]

Address [   ]

[   ]   Post code [   ][   ][   ][   ][   ][   ]

Tel: [   ]   Fax: [   ]

Starting date in this position: [   ]   Finishing date in this position: [   ]

Page no.: **2 of 3**

123

Becor House, Green Lane, Lincoln LN6 7DL
T 0870 703 9009 F 0870 751 5552

The **online resource** For**Landlords**

7. Additional information
This section should be completed by the **Tenant**

Use this space to provide any additional information we may have requested. If you run out of space, please use a separate sheet.

8. Declaration
This section should be completed by the **Tenant**

Please read the declaration and sign below. WE CANNOT PROCEED WITH THIS APPLICATION IF YOU DO NOT SIGN.

I hereby confirm that the information provided by me is to the best of my knowledge true. I consent to this information being verified by contacting the third parties detailed in this form. I understand that the results of the findings will be forwarded to the appointed letting agent and/or landlord and may be accessed again should I default on my rental payment or apply for a new tenancy agreement in the future. I agree that ForLandlords or their approved agent may search the files of a Credit Reference Agency and IDS Ltd, the insurance industry's data collection agency, which will keep a record of that search. I understand that I may request the name and address of the Credit Reference Agency to whom I may then apply for a copy of the information provided.

I also understand that in the event of my defaulting on the rental payment, that any such default may be recorded with the Credit Referencing Agency and IDS Ltd, who may supply the information to other credit companies or insurers in the quest for the responsible granting of tenancies, insurance and credit.

I understand that in the event of any default by me in respect of the covenants in my tenancy agreement with my landlord, the information contained herein may be disclosed to ForLandlords and/or one or more tracing companies and/or debt collection agencies in order to recover any monies due or to trace my whereabouts. I understand that the information provided by me may be transferred to a country outside of the EU for the purposes only of processing this referencing application, notwithstanding such transfer, ForLandlords will remain the Data Controller for the purposes of this application.

The information provided in this form by me is information as described in Ground 17 of the Housing Act 1996 and I understand that if any information within this application is found to be untrue, it is grounds for termination of the tenancy. I also understand that any default in the payment of rent may affect any future application for tenancies, credit or insurance and that the assessment of this application presumes that at some time during the tenancy agreement, I may be granted or allowed some form of deferred payment.

Signed:

Name: Date:

The details you provide, including your email address, will be held by ForLandlords and the letting agent and may be used to keep you up to date on our products and services and those of Hanover Park Services plc and other organizations we believe will be of interest to you. If you prefer not to receive this information, please tick this box: ☐

ForLandlords is a trading name of Hanover Park Services plc | Registered address: Phoenix House, 11 Wellesley Road, Croydon, CR0 2NW
Company Registration No: 04194617 | Hanover Park Services plc is a member of the General Insurance Standards Council

Page no.: **3 of 3**

124

Glossary

Note: This glossary must be considered within the context of property letting and, particularly, in relation to assured shorthold tenancies unless otherwise defined.

Accelerated possession. A fast-track legal procedure for seeking possession through the courts in England and Wales.

Affidavit. A statement of fact made in writing and verified by oath, before someone with the authority to administer it (usually a solicitor).

Assign. The transfer of legal title or interest, for example a tenant passing their entitlement to occupy a property to another person. Assignment is usually prohibited by the tenancy agreement.

Assured shorthold tenancy. A tenancy defined by the Housing Act 1988 (as amended by the Housing Act 1996) granted by a landlord to a tenant for a fixed period. This is the most common form of residential tenancy in England and Wales. Landlords can obtain possession of their property (after six months through the courts), if they wish, subject to the fixed-term expiring and proper notice being issued.

Assured tenancy. A tenancy defined by the Housing Act 1988 (as amended by the Housing Act 1996) granted by a private landlord to a private tenant in England and Wales. Assured tenants have the right to remain in the property unless the landlord can prove to the court that there are grounds for possession. There is no automatic right to possession when the tenancy ends.

Bailiff. An officer of the court with the authority to enforce possession orders.

Bank draft. A secure form of payment that looks like a cheque but is guaranteed by the payee's bank.

Break clause. A clause in a tenancy agreement that allows the tenant and/or the landlord the right to bring the tenancy to an end before its normal expiry date. Break clauses usually specify the conditions and notice period required.

British Standard. The display of a British Standard number (e.g. BS 1234) on, for example, a consumer product, shows that the manufacturer claims to have made it in accordance with the British Standard. If accompanied by the letters EN and/or ISO, it was developed as a (EN) European or (ISO) international standard, then adopted by the UK as a British Standard.

Buy-to-let. A scheme originally promoted by ARLA (Association of Residential Letting Agents) which eventually introduced mortgages designed specifically for landlords. Most banks and building societies now offer variations of this type of loan. The maximum loan-to-value (LTV) is often lower but, unlike an ordinary mortgage, rental income is taken into consideration by the lender when calculating the amount offered.

Capital gains tax. A liability incurred, according to the level of profit gained, when an increase in property value has been realised. An individual's permanent home is usually exempt, but additional homes and letting-units are not.

Capital growth. The rise in value of a property over time.

Carbon monoxide. An odourless invisible poisonous gas (CO_1) produced through the incomplete combustion of carbon-based fuels. Yellow-coloured or smoky gas-fire and gas-boiler flames suggest the presence of CO_1 and their operation should be discontinued immediately to prevent potentially fatal consequences.

Company let. A letting to a company (rather than an individual) cannot be 'assured' under the Housing Act 1988 and, as a result, such tenants generally have less security of tenure. Company-let agreements are widely available and create a usually straightforward contractual arrangement between landlord and tenant.

Contract. A legally binding agreement between two or more parties.

CORGI. The Council for Registered Gas Installers. Engineers who conduct gas-safety inspections for landlords must be registered.

Counterpart agreement. A duplicate of the tenancy agreement, retained by the landlord and having the tenant's signature on it (the tenant retains the agreement containing the landlord's signature).

Covenant. A promise made in a legal document which can be positive or restrictive (for example, making it an obligation to perform or, conversely, prohibit certain actions).

Demised premises. The part or parts of the property where the tenant or lessee has legal right to exclusive possession.

Deposit. A sum held as security against certain events and for a set period. The 'events' might include rent arrears, damage, loss, and the reinstatement of decoration and cleanliness (fair wear and tear excluded). The tenancy agreement normally specifies which events are covered by the deposit and whether interest will be paid. From 6 April 2007, all deposits collected by landlords or letting-agents from assured shorthold tenants must be protected by a government-approved scheme. The rules of the relevant scheme must be incorporated into the tenancy agreement to prevent one set of legal obligations conflicting with the other.

Dilapidations. This refers to a state of disrepair for which the tenant is legally accountable. The tenancy agreement should describe the extent of the tenant's liability and the landlord must have suffered or will suffer financial loss due to the disrepair. The cost of dilapidations is usually deducted from the tenant's deposit at the end of the tenancy.

Display label. All new furniture must carry a display label at the point of sale, except mattresses and bed-bases, pillows, cushions and seat pads, loose covers and stretch covers. These labels provide information about the product's compliance with the 1988 safety regulations.

Eviction. The process by which a tenant is prevented or removed from physical possession of the property. Legal eviction can only be performed with a court order and by officers approved by the court.

Exclusive possession. A legal right to occupy the property and exclude others from it.

Express obligations. These are the promises made by tenant and landlord within the terms of the tenancy agreement. They are secondary to **implied obligations** imposed by common law and statute.

Fair wear and tear. The normal day-to-day deterioration of decoration, furnishings and fittings, that occur over time and are distinct from dilapidations. Tenants are not usually made liable for fair wear and tear.

Fittings. These are usually mobile items or things that can be removed easily from the property, not forming part of the structure or fabric of the dwelling.

Fixtures. These are 'fixed' elements, the removal of which would be likely to cause damage to the fabric of walls, ceilings, floors, windows or doors.

Forfeiture. The tenant 'forfeits' their tenancy when a landlord brings it to an end because of a breach of the terms, for example, due to the non-payment of rent. Although under certain circumstances and following a set procedure, the landlord has the right to bring the tenancy to an end, the tenant cannot be evicted without an order from the court.

Freehold. A property and/or land held indefinitely (owned forever) with no other person or agency having greater interest.

Furnished. There is no legal definition of what constitutes a furnished dwelling. However, tenants looking for 'furnished' property generally expect all of the following items to be supplied: seating, beds, wardrobes, tables, white goods, light fittings, carpets and curtains.

Gas flue. An installation through which the waste gases of combustion pass to the exterior of the property. Most modern gas appliances require a flue.

Gas safety certificate. A document issued by a CORGI registered installer confirming the inspection and safety of gas installations, flues and appliances, and their associated pipework. Copies of the certificate must be given to each new tenant *before* occupation *and* within 28 days of an inspection being undertaken. Testing must be conducted annually.

Gearing. The process whereby investors use property as security to acquire funding, so that further properties can be purchased. Gearing brings a better return when the total yield plus capital growth exceeds the borrowing rate.

Gross rental income. The total income from letting the property before deductions for tax and expenditure.

Grounds for possession. The 17 'grounds' contained in the Housing Act 1988 (as amended by the Housing Act 1996) through which landlords can apply to court for possession of their property. Mandatory grounds are those where the court must grant a possession order providing the ground is proved. Discretionary grounds are those where the court can take other matters into consideration before considering whether to grant a possession order.

Guarantor. Someone who agrees to accept the liability for some or all of the tenant's obligations if the tenant defaults on rent payments or other terms of tenancy.

Headlessor. The individual, company, group, institution or agency, who establish, govern and apply the terms of a lease upon the lessees of leasehold properties.

HM Revenue & Customs. The government agency responsible for the collection of tax and, where required, the inspection of accounts.

Holding over. A situation where a tenant remains in occupation despite the tenancy having ended or expiry of the term having passed and with no new tenancy or term being granted.

Housing benefit. An allowance available to those on low income and who satisfy the criteria. Housing benefit (H/b) is intended to pay for all or some of the rent. It is funded by government and administered by local authorities. Applicants can request a **pre-tenancy determination** to be undertaken by the rent officer service prior to considering a tenancy from a private landlord.

Housing Acts. These are the Acts of Parliament containing the definitions and rules for private residential letting in England and Wales. The 1980 Act first introduced the **shorthold** concept. The 1985 Act consolidated various statutory provisions and provided a definition for 'houses in multiple occupation'. The 1988 Act introduced assured and assured shorthold tenancies. The 1996 Act refined the existing provisions, removed the notice requirement for creating shorthold tenancies, and improved the landlord's possession rights. The 2004 Act introduced mandatory HiMO licensing for certain types of property, together with a new HiMO definition and a more stringent regime of health and safety requirements. It also provided a route through which legislators can introduce compulsory tenancy deposit schemes.

Implied obligations. The rights of tenants and landlords provided by common law and statute, contained in all leases, even if they are not written into the agreement. For example, all tenants have a right to **quiet enjoyment** of the demised premises they occupy. If an implied obligation is not specified in the terms of tenancy, then the 'usual covenant' will apply, with reference to the tenant's or landlord's right under common law or statute.

Improvements. The Landlord and Tenant Act 1985 makes landlords responsible for certain **repairs**, providing the tenancy has a fixed term of seven years or less. A repair is the reinstatement, restoration or fixing of something that is faulty. An improvement goes beyond a repair and is not usually an allowable letting expense when calculating tax.

Income tax. The liability of landlords to pay the HM Revenue & Customs a portion of rental income profit, based on total income, over and above any personal allowance and less any permitted expenses.

Insurance. A policy that offers protection for various eventualities in return for a payment. Landlords and tenants can obtain policies to protect rent and provide legal services, in addition to the more traditional buildings and contents provision. Most domestic policies offer inadequate terms for letting and landlords should read them carefully to ensure sufficient cover is afforded.

Intranet. A restricted version of the internet with access and information limited to a company or organisation and its employees.

Inventory clerk. A specialist who can be employed to create an inventory at the start of tenancy and offer an independent assessment of dilapidations at the end of the term.

Inventory. A record and schedule of the existence and condition of furnishings, fittings, fixtures, appliances, equipment and decoration, provided by a landlord at the start of tenancy, and used to assess dilapidations when the tenancy ends.

Joint tenancy. This is where two or more people are named as tenants on the same tenancy agreement. Joint tenants are usually **severally liable** for the rent and equally culpable for any breach of tenancy terms.

Landlord and Tenant Act. The 1985 Act consolidated the prior Landlord and

Tenant Act, Housing Act and Rent Act provisions. This piece of legislation includes details of the landlord's repairing obligation and the right of tenants to information about their landlord's identity and address.

Landlord. The person, persons, company, organisation or institution who provide all or part of a property to be used and/or occupied by a tenant, usually in return for rent.

Lease. Strictly, a lease is the same as a tenancy. However, it is commonly used to describe the document an owner (more correctly, the lessee) of a leasehold property receives at the point of purchase. It specifies their rights and covenants and the period of time they can occupy and/or use the building.

Leasehold. Property that is subject to a lease.

Lessee. The person who is granted a lease by the lessor.

Lessor. The person who grants the lease to a lessee.

Licence. A licence to occupy is often given when a tenancy cannot be created, for example, where the tenant does not have exclusive use of any part of the accommodation. Licensees generally have less security of tenure than assured or assured shorthold tenants.

Management charge. A mandatory fee imposed in return for management services. Leasehold properties with common parts often have a management charge associated with them for services, such as the upkeep of external parts, cleaning and decoration of communal hallways, building insurance and garden maintenance, accounting and agency provisions.

Minor. A person under the age of 18 who cannot legally be bound by contract.

Mortgage broker. An intermediary who identifies and advises on the best value mortgages available and deals with the administration involved, in return for a fee. Brokers do not sell their own products and those offered may be restricted in volume and variety.

Mortgage. In theory, a loan granted to assist with the purchase of property; in practice, a mortgagee does not own the property outright until the loan is repaid and instead becomes the lessee, hence the mortgage company has the right to repossess the property if payments are not maintained.

Multiple occupation. A house in multiple occupation is defined in the Housing Act 2004 as meaning a building, or part of a building (e.g. a flat):

◆ which is occupied by more than one household and in which more than one household shares an amenity (or the building lacks an amenity) such as a bathroom, toilet or cooking facilities; or

◆ which is occupied by more than one household and which is a converted building which does not entirely comprise self-contained flats (whether or not there is also a sharing or lack of amenities); or

◆ which comprises entirely of converted self-contained flats and the standard of conversion does not meet, at a minimum, that required by the 1991 Building Regulation and more than one third of the flats are occupied under short tenancies.

And is 'occupied' by more than one household:

◆ as their only or main residence, or
◆ as a refuge by persons escaping domestic violence, or
◆ during term time by students, or
◆ for some other purpose that is prescribed in regulations.

And the households comprise:

◆ families (including foster children, children being cared for) and current domestic employees,
◆ single persons,
◆ co-habiting couples (whether or not of the same sex).

Net rental income. The income gained from a let property after deducting expenses.

Non-resident. For tax purposes, a non-resident landlord (NRL) is one who lets property in the United Kingdom but lives overseas for six months or more. Unless the NRL has received an exemption certificate from HM Revenue & Customs, their letting-agent (or tenant if there is no agent) must deduct the landlord's tax from the rent at the basic rate and make payment on his behalf.

Notice. A formal process telling the tenant that their tenancy will end on a predetermined date, which may include details about the landlord's intention to seek possession through the court if the tenant fails to vacate.

Permanent label. All new furniture (except those mentioned under **display label** above) must have a permanent label fixed to it, describing the product's compliance with the 1988 Regulations and information about the foam content.

Prescribed form. A term given that demands some forms and/or notices must have a layout and/or wording that conforms with the legislation describing it. For example, a landlord's **Notice to Quit** has to contain certain information, without which it may be considered invalid by the court.

Pre-tenancy determination. Those who qualify for housing benefit can request a pre-tenancy determination (PTD) when considering a tenancy from a private landlord. A PTD is arranged by the local authority via the rent officer service and provides an indication of the maximum benefit that will be paid for the property. A recipient is then aware of whether the entire rent or only a portion of it will be covered. PTDs are applied to the property, not the H/b claimant, and are valid for 12 months.

Quiet enjoyment. The tenant's statutory right to occupy and use the property within the terms agreed and without interference or disturbance.

Reinstatement. Restoring something to its former state. With regard to property letting, this usually means repairing to make-good or replacing or renewing to a level of quality commensurate with when it was first supplied, i.e. at the start of tenancy.

Rent Officer. The Rent Officer Service is an Executive Agency of the Department of the Environment, Transport and the Regions, and operates through local authorities. The Rent Officer's main functions are to undertake Fair Rent evaluations for regulated and secure tenancies, to make pre-tenancy determinations for housing benefit, and advise local authorities about the effects on rent of Housing Renovation Grant applications.

Rent. Rent is normally a sum of money paid under contract, by a tenant, in return for possession of a property for a period of time. However, rent *can* mean something other than legal tender, for example, it may be agreed that a service is provided instead.

Resident. A resident landlord is one who lives in the same building as their tenant. An exception exists where the landlord lives in a purpose-built block of flats and lets one of the other flats in the same block.

Roll-over relief. The term refers to delaying the payment of Capital Gains Tax by reinvesting the profit made from the sale of one business into another.

Security of tenure. The right of the tenant to **quiet enjoyment** of the property for a determined or indefinite period of time.

Service charge. A mandatory charge made by a landlord or headlessor to the tenant or leaseholder.

Set-off. Tenants have a right, under certain conditions, to withhold rent for repairs that have been requested but not conducted. They can set off the appropriate sum to finance the repairs they have had to arrange themselves as a result.

Severally liable. Joint tenants are usually described as being severally liable. This means each tenant is equally responsible and accountable for the other tenants' actions. For example, if one tenant fails to pay rent, it is the same as if all tenants had failed to make the payment.

Short assured tenancy. A tenancy in Scotland under the Housing (Scotland) Act 1988 and similar to (but not the same as) the assured shorthold tenancy in England and Wales.

Sitting tenant. Someone whose occupation of a property is protected by law, even if the property is sold to another person.

Stamp Duty Land Tax. The Finance Act inflicts Stamp Duty Land Tax on the *net present value* of rent payable under a lease or tenancy.

Statutory periodic tenancy. A statutory periodic tenancy (SPT) is created automatically at the end of an assured shorthold tenancy (AST) if either the landlord or tenant do nothing to prevent it. An SPT has the same terms as the prior AST but runs according to the periodic nature of rent payments, for example, month to month.

Statutory protection. The rights and security afforded to both landlord and tenant by primary legislation under Acts of Law (as distinct from contrary terms that may be written into a tenancy agreement).

Sub-let. The term given to a tenant who lets the property (or part of it) to another tenant.

Succession. The right of a spouse or a family member who satisfies the criteria to continue enjoying occupation of a property, after the tenant has died. Family members *can* include unmarried partners, regardless of gender, if a court interprets the relationship accordingly.

Surrender. A tenant who voluntarily relinquishes their tenancy in agreement with the landlord.

Survey. The examination of a building and the identification of faults and/or an appraisal of current market value.

Template. A stencil or pattern used as a guide to create a similar product or consummate document.

Tenancy agreement. A contractually binding agreement between landlord and tenant, detailing the terms under which a property is provided. Verbal agreements should be avoided as they give rise to doubt and the terms will be difficult to prove in court.

Tenancy. The exclusive possession of property usually granted for a period of time and in return for rent.

Tenant. Someone with a legal right to occupy and/or use a property according to certain terms and conditions.

Unfurnished. There is no legal definition of what constitutes an unfurnished property. Generally it means the dwelling is supplied without furnishings, fittings, appliances and equipment, but may include fixtures.

Vacant possession. The property is handed over at completion with no one occupying it and no one having any legal right to occupy it.

Vendor. The person selling the property.

Void period. The period between tenancies when the property is empty and there is therefore no rental income.

White goods. A term that refers to kitchen appliances such as an automatic washing-machine, fridge-freezer, dishwasher and cooker.

Yield. The annual rate of return on investment expressed as a percentage.

Useful Information

ARLA (Association of Residential Letting Agents), Maple House, 53-55 Woodside Road, Amersham, Bucks HP6 6AA. Tel: 0845 345 5752. Website: **www.arla.co.uk**

British Insurance Brokers Association, 14 Bevis Marks, London EC3A 7NT. Tel: (consumer helpline) 0901 814 0015. Website: **www.biba.org.uk**

British Standards Institute, 389 Chiswick High Road, London W4 4AL. Tel: 020 8996 9001. Website: **bsi-global.com**

British Urban Regeneration Association, 63–66 Hatton Garden, London EC1N 8LE. Tel: 0800 0181 260. Website: **www.bura.org.uk**

Communities and Local Government (formally the Office of the Deputy Prime Minister – free letting literature), Eland House, Bressenden Place, London SW1E 5DU. Tel: (helpline) 020 7944 4400. Website: **www.communities.gov.uk**

CORGI (Council of Registered Gas Installers), 1 Elmwood, Chineham Business Park, Crockford Lane, Basingstoke, Hampshire RG24 8WG. Tel: 0800 915 0485. Website: **www.trustcorgi.com**

Court Service (Information and Advice), Customer Service Unit, 5th Floor, Clive House, Petty France, London SW1H 9EX. Tel: 0845 456 8770. Website: **www.hmcourts-service.gov.uk**

DBERR – Department for Business, Enterprise and Regulatory Reform (formally the DTI), 1 Victoria Street, London SW1H 0ET. Tel: 020 7215 5000. Website: **www.berr.gov.uk**

Deposit Protection Service (Free Custodial Scheme), The Pavilions, Bridgwater Road, Bristol BS99 6AA. Tel: 0870 7071 707. Website: **www.depositprotection.com**

DWP (Department for Work and Pensions) formally the DSS, Public

Enquiry Office, Room 112, The Adelphi, 1–11 John Adam Street, London WC2N 6HT. Tel: 020 7712 2171. Website: **www.dwp.gov.uk**

Federation of Small Businesses, Sir Frank Whittle Way, Blackpool Business Park, Blackpool, Lancashire FY4 2FE. Tel: 01253 336000. Website: **www.fsb.org.uk**

FSA (The Financial Services Authority), 25 The North Colonnade, Canary Wharf, London E14 5HS. Tel: 0845 606 1234. Website: **www.moneymadeclear.fsa.gov.uk**

Health and Safety Executive, Rose Court, 2 Southwark Bridge, London SE1 9HS. Tel: 0845 345 0055 (InfoLine). Website: **www.hse.gov.uk**

HM Revenue & Customs. Find details of your local tax office enquiry centre or ask questions about self-assessment. Tel: 0845 9000 444. Website: **www.hmrc.gov.uk**

Information Commissioner (Data Protection), Wycliffe House, Water Lane, Wilmslow, Cheshire SK9 5AF. Tel: 01625 545 745. Website: **www.informationcommissioner.gov.uk**

Leasehold Advisory Service, 31 Worship Street, London EC2A 2DX. Tel: 020 7374 5380. Website: **www.lease-advice.org.uk**

National Association of Citizens Advice Bureaux, Myddelton House, 115-123 Pentonville Road, London N1 9LZ. Tel: 020 7833 2181. Website: **www.citizensadvice.org.uk**

National Grid, The (Gas Emergency Service), Warwick Technology Park, Gallows Hill, Warwick CV34 6DA. Tel: 0845 605 6677 (emergency 0800 111999). Website: **www.nationalgrid.com/uk**

Office of Fair Trading, Fleetbank House, 2–6 Salisbury Square, London EC4Y 8JX. Tel: 08457 224499. Website: **www.oft.gov.uk**

Office of Fair Trading (Scotland), 23 Walker Street, Edinburgh EH3 7HX. Tel: 0131 220 5930. Website: **www.oft.gov.uk**

Office of Public Sector Information (ex-HMSO). Legislation, statutory instruments and other parliamentary documents can be downloaded from here. See The Stationery Office (TSO) contact details for purchasable copies. Website: **www.opsi.gov.uk**

OFWAT (Office of Water Services – Regulator of the Water Industry), Centre City Tower, 7 Hill Street, Birmingham B5 4UA. Tel: 0121 625 1300. Website: **www.ofwat.gov.uk**

Rent Service, The, 5 Welbeck Street, London W1G 9YQ. Tel. 020 7023 6000. Website: **www.therentservice.gov.uk**

Royal Institute of Chartered Surveyors (RICS), Contact Centre, Surveyor Court, Westwood Way, Coventry CV4 8JE. Tel: 0870 333 1600. Website: **www.rics.org**

Scottish Executive Development Department (free leaflets), Victoria Quay, Edinburgh EH6 6QQ. Tel: 08457 741 741.
  Website: **www.scotland.gov.uk/housing/leaflets**

Tenancy Deposit Scheme (Insurance-Based Scheme), The Dispute Service Ltd, PO Box 541, Amersham, Bucks HP6 6ZR. Tel: 0845 226 7837.
  Website: **www.thedisputeservice.co.uk**

Tenancy Deposit Solutions (Insurance-Based Scheme), 3rd Floor, Kingmaker House, Station Road, New Barnet, Hertfordshire EN5 1NZ.
  Tel: 0871 703 0552. Website: **www.mydeposits.co.uk**

Trading Standards, 4–5 Hadleigh Business Centre, 351 London Road, Hadleigh, Essex SS17 2BT. Tel: 0870 872 9000.
  Website: **www.tradingstandards.gov.uk**

TSO (The Stationery Office), TSO Orders Post/Cash Dept., PO Box 29, Norwich NR3 1GN. Tel: 0870 600 5522. Website: **www.tso.co.uk**

Valuation Office (Council Tax), Chief Executives Office, New Court, 48 Carey Street, London WC2A 2JE. Tel: 020 7506 1700. Website: **www.voa.gov.uk**

LANDLORDS' ASSOCIATIONS

Cornwall Residential Landlords Association, C/O Follett Stock, Truro Business Park, Truro, Cornwall TR4 9NH. Tel: 01872 241700.
  Website: **www.crla.org.uk**

Darlington & District Private Landlords Association, 94 Cleveland Terrace, Darlington, DL3 8HR. Tel: 07723 389664.
  Website: **www.darlingtonlandlords.co.uk**

Dorset Landlords Association (now a branch of the National Landlords Association), DRLA, PO Box 4840, Wimborne BH21 3WZ.
  Tel: 01202 640236. Website: **www.drla.co.uk**

Eastern Landlords Association, Suite A, St Francis House, 141–147 Queens Road, Norwich NR1 3PN. Tel: 01603 767101.
  Website: **www.easternlandlords.org.uk**

East Lindsey Landlords' Association, 8 Jordan Grove, Sutton on Sea, Lincs LN12 2FJ. Tel: 01507 441869. Website: **www.landlordsassociation.org**

East Midlands Property Owners, 78 Lenton Boulevard, Lenton, Nottingham NG7 2EN. Tel: 0845 094 0386. Website: **www.empo.co.uk**

Fife Landlords Association, Caledonian House, Links Road, Leven, Fife KY8 4HS. Tel: 0778 755 3272. Website: **www.fifelandlords.org**

Gateshead Private Landlords Association, Millennium House, 207 Coatsworth Road, Gateshead, Tyne and Wear NE8 1SR.
  Tel: 0191 433 6699. Website: **www.renting-in-gateshead.co.uk**

Gloucestershire Landlords Association, Peter Whitestone, Applehurst, Lowbands, Redmarley D'Abitot, Gloucestershire GL19 3NF. Tel: 01452 840587. Website: **www.gloslet.com**

Hull & District Landlords' Association, 56 Cottingham Road, Hull HU6. Tel: 01482 353072. Website: **www.hdla.net**

Landlords Association for Northern Ireland, LANI, 257 Lisburn Road, Belfast BT9 7EN. Tel: 028 9066 7233. Website: **www.lani.org.uk**

National Federation of Residential Landlords, 8 Wellington House, Camden Street, Portslade, East Sussex BN41 1DU. Tel: 0845 456 9313. Website: **www.nfrl.org.uk**

National Landlords Association, 22–26 Albert Embankment, London SE1 7TJ. Tel: 020 7840 8937. Website: **www.landlords.org.uk**

North Cumbria Landlords' Association, 61 Durdar Road, Carlisle CA2 4SB. Tel: 01228 536465. Website: **www.carlislerentedaccommodation.co.uk**

North Staffordshire Landlords' Association, PO Box 1564, Stoke-on-Trent ST1 3TW. Tel: 01782 279238. Website: **www.nsla.co.uk**

North Wales Private Landlords Association, NWPLA, PO Box 36, Rhyl LL18 1ZD. Tel: 01745 330792. Website: see **www.nfrl.org.uk**

North West Landlords Association Limited, 113 Tongue Moor Road, Bolton, Lancashire BL2 2DL. Tel: 0845 345 1386. Website: **www.nwla.co.uk**

North West Property Owners Association, Freepost NWW131A, PO Box 80, Liverpool L23 6YJ. Tel: 0845 456 1659. Website: **www.nwpoa.co.uk**

Residential Landlords Association, 1 Roebuck Lane, Sale, Manchester M33 7SY. Tel: 0845 666 5000. Website: **www.rla.org.uk**

Scottish Association of Landlords, 20 Forth Street, Edinburgh EH1 3LH. Tel: 0131 270 4774. Website: **www.scottishlandlords.com**

Sheffield & District Landlord Association, SADLA, PO Box 3199, Sheffield S11 7WR. Tel: 0114 2960670. Website: **www.sadla.org.uk**

South Ayrshire Landlords' Association, 1 Whittle Road, Ayr KA8 9PY. Tel: 01292 612083.

South Devon Residential Landlords Association, 141 St Marychurch Road, Torquay, Devon TQ1 3HW. Tel: 01803 314750. Website: **www.devon-landlords.com**

Southern Private Landlords Association, 8 Wellington House, Camden Street, Portslade BN41 1DU. Tel: 01273 600847. Website (linked to NFRL): **www.spla.co.uk**

South West Landlords Association, SWLA, 12 Radnor Place, Plymouth PL4 8DW. Tel: 01752 510913. Website: **www.landlordssouthwest.co.uk**

Westcountry Landlords' Association, PO Box 454, Plymouth PL3 4WL.

Tel: 01752 242980. Website: **www.wlainfo.co.uk**

Weymouth & District Private Landlords Association, 94 The Esplanade, Weymouth, Dorset DT4 7AT. Tel: 01305 767327.

Wrekin Landlords' Association, 9B Churchill Buildings, Queen Street, Wellington, Telford TF1 1SN. Tel: 01952 727322.
Website: **www.wrekinlandlords.co.uk**

York Residential Landlords' Association, Sinclair House, Main Street, Heslington, York YO10 5EB. Tel: 07050 367504.
Website: **www.yorkrla.com**

Yorkshire Coast Residential Landlords Association, PO Box 227, Scarborough YO11 1YW. Tel: 0845 330 4582. Website: **www.ycrla.com**

ADDITIONAL WEBSITES

www.buytolet.co.uk A site run by ARLA (Association of Residential Letting Agents) devoted to the purchasing of residential property specifically to let it out.

www.landlordlaw.co.uk Superb legal information resource for landlords with access to tenancy documents.

www.landlordzone.co.uk My personal favourite – contains a wealth of information and helpful resources.

www.letlink.co.uk The Letting Centre site has a vast amount of valuable information and advice.

www.letting-network.com Contains links to other useful landlord resource sites.

www.propertysecrets.net A fabulous site for all property investors – this resource also contains over 100 articles associated with property investment and buy-to-let written by yours truly.

www.scottishlaw.org.uk View the laws and regulations affecting landlords operating in Scotland.

www.themoneycentre.co.uk Advice and analysis of the best buy-to-let mortgages available.

www.themovechannel.com Guidance for novice landlords and resources for anyone moving home.

Index